T0267293

GARRETT GUNDERSON

MONEY
UNMA$KED

UNLEARN, UNLOCK, &
TAKE BACK CONTROL OF
YOUR FINANCES & LIFE

GREENLEAF
BOOK GROUP PRESS

Published by Greenleaf Book Group Press
Austin, Texas
www.gbgpress.com

Distributed by Greenleaf Book Group

For ordering information or special discounts for bulk purchases, please contact Greenleaf Book Group at PO Box 91869, Austin, TX 78709, 512.891.6100.

Design and composition by Greenleaf Book Group and Teresa Muñiz
Cover design by Greenleaf Book Group and Teresa Muñiz
For permission credits, please see page 189, which is a continuation of the copyright page.

Publisher's Cataloging-in-Publication data is available.

Print ISBN: 979-8-88645-059-0

eBook ISBN: 979-8-88645-060-6

To offset the number of trees consumed in the printing of our books, Greenleaf donates a portion of the proceeds from each printing to the Arbor Day Foundation. Greenleaf Book Group has replaced over 50,000 trees since 2007.

Printed in the United States of America on acid-free paper

23 24 25 26 27 28 29 30   10 9 8 7 6 5 4 3 2 1

First Edition

I dedicate this to the dreamers, healers, and givers who deliver value through art and invention, expression, and creation. With all my love.

Contents

What's Your Number?

"When health is absent, wisdom can't reveal itself,
art cannot be manifest, strength cannot be exerted,
wealth is useless, and reason is powerless."

—HEROPHILOS, 300 BCE

"What would you do with a billion dollars?"

It was on a flight with my business partner, Les McGuire, when one of us asked the question. I don't remember who said it; we had a habit of challenging each other philosophically. I do remember once I took the time to consider the question, it floored me.

I had no idea what I would do with a billion dollars.

And I had no idea because I couldn't figure out how to *earn* a billion dollars.

Before my brain would let me dream of the things I could buy or the Main Streets I could save, I had to see the path to a billion. And I didn't have a clue how to do that.

At the time, I was in my twenties and committed to the hustle and grind. Our company, Engenuity, helped people get their financial houses in order. We held events, met with clients one-on-one, and had a subscription with newsletters, audios, and daily resources to help people take control over their finances. My life was all about numbers: getting more clients so I could hit my target revenue. So why couldn't I wrap my head around that big number?

What strategy would get me to a billion? The question haunted me as I drove home from the airport. If I couldn't figure that out, even in theory, what did that say about me, about my value? That thought set off a chain reaction of self-defeating thoughts:

You are insignificant.

You aren't doing anything of consequence.

You are worthless.

From there, it was a swift descent into feeling depressed. I remember I stopped at the convenience store and bought a huge bag of Laffy Taffy. That night, I watched reruns on TV and ate all the candy and felt terrible about myself. Pretty sexy existential crisis, eating taffy and binge-watching *Friends* all night.

Then, somewhere between Ross and Rachel arguing about breaking up and Ross and Rachel arguing about getting back together, it hit me: *I don't know how to earn a billion dollars because I don't know what I would* do *with a billion dollars.*

Ah, the paradox. I was right back where I started.

I couldn't fathom how I would be a steward over that much money. And because I couldn't even imagine that, it was impossible for me to come up with a strategy to earn it. I had been more focused on my goals than on my value. On my activity over my vision.

That realization started to substantially change my thinking. I became curious about how our clients were feeling about their lives. So many people we worked with had some arbitrary number they had to reach to feel okay with themselves. I also had numbers in my mind. These numbers in my bank, or on my balance sheet, were required before having kids, before buying a home, before considering myself successful, before considering myself okay.

Over the next few months, during our quarterly meetings with clients, I noticed a pattern. No matter what we did for them financially, no matter how much money they earned, our clients' stories didn't change much at all. They were still feeling they should be further ahead, they were still in the struggle, and they still didn't have *enough*. For those who hit their arbitrary number, they found it rarely provided happiness, contentment, or relief because they compared themselves to others who had more.

More.

It's an ever-moving target that fuels the impossible, unwinnable game. There is always someone with more. Happy with a 30 percent return on investment? Sure. Unless their neighbor had a 34 percent return; now they were pissed. Are you kidding me? Thirty percent is awesome—nothing to be pissed about. And yet, because of the game of more, the game of comparison, they weren't satisfied.

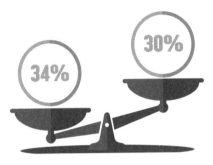

It was the same for me. Comparison is a powerful motivator, but it never ends. Acquiring stuff, achieving status, adding zeros to your bank account—these things made me feel good, for a moment. As a result, I began to understand that accumulating money just for the sake of having it wasn't enough of a motivator.

I came to believe we were renting happiness, paying for fleeting moments with our health, our relationships, and our enjoyment of life.

Then I began to wonder, What would our clients do with a billion dollars? Could they answer the question? My guess was, probably not. I still couldn't answer it myself, but I kept thinking about it. And thinking about it.

What amount of money would be enough?

What amount of money would provide true freedom? And can money even provide such a thing?

What amount of money would be meaningful and provide lasting happiness?

What amount of money would unlock a new financial destiny, one that would help me, and others, build a life we could love?

What amount was the right number, the magic number?

The Misinformation That Shapes Our Lives

I'm a coal miner's son, as was my father before me. My great-grandfather was born in Italy into a life of scarcity and sacrifice. He carried those wounds with him and passed them down to his children, who passed them down to his children, and then on down to my sisters and me. In my book *Disrupting Sacred Cows*, I share how the fears, beliefs, and values around money handed down to me shaped me. Because of my inherited scarcity mindset, I pinched pennies and hoarded money like a prepper storing supplies for the apocalypse.

I also inherited my family's work ethic, which, combined with a scarcity mindset, caused me to spend most of my time working to earn as much money as possible. Saving money and making money were my primary goals.

We have different pasts, but you have your own inherited fears, beliefs, and values around money, and I'm willing to bet you a pound of my favorite coffee that you also inherited a scarcity mindset. You see, it's an epidemic. The world we live in is fueled by it.

> The belief that resources are scarce is by far the greatest destroyer of wealth.

To be clear, I'm not suggesting that poverty isn't real, that a good percentage of the planet does not have access to enough food and water or adequate health care. In fact, our scarcity thinking perpetuates this problem. If we continue to believe that we need to hang on to our share of the resources, people will continue to suffer.

But it is through this lens that we rarely create wealth, seldom chose love, and often become selfish. We are selfish when we think only of what's in it for us. Or when we feel like victims or become entitled.

The concept of scarcity is misleading. It's a belief that there is only so much to go around, that we have to sacrifice to succeed, and that money is value, *our* value. Scarcity is hard to detect for most, because it becomes familiar, like a companion. That companion is what we know, what we see, what we hear, and even how we feel. It is as invisible as air and as suffocating as carbon dioxide—hard to detect, but deadly. Scarcity is reinforced on the news and social media. It is a common language of competition, division, and even defeat.

Scarcity is in our words and embedded in our phrases:

I don't.

I can't.

There isn't enough.

Enough.

Who decides what is enough? Will we have enough? Can I provide enough? Am I good enough? Have I sacrificed enough?

It is through the avenue of sacrifice that scarcity grows; it lives in our emotions, and it permeates every aspect of being. It's in the lyrics of our music, the voice in our head, and the memes of our life. It has defined our culture.

It's clichéd but powerful. Persuasive, but untrue.

In scarcity we ignore resourcefulness, collaboration, and innovation. Scarcity begs us to take what is ours or hold on to what we have because you can never have enough.

Enough.

In scarcity the only solution to enough is more. It is never enough; there is always more. More comes from others.

Taking.

Working.

Hustling.

More is the vernacular that feeds the scarcity hunger inside. Disguised as protection and providing, thoughts of more are lies and thieves.

Taking our energy.

Stealing our time.

Tugging at our emotions, telling us we can be at peace eventually, but only after other things are complete.

A bigger retirement account.

A certain amount in the bank.

Or the next promotion, award, or accolade.

More.

More.

More.

Wanting more security, more money, more time.

Well, more of anything. Robbing us of what is most divine.

Our Soul Purpose.
Our life.

Keeping us in the constant struggle where there can never be enough, until we finally say . . .

ENOUGH IS ENOUGH.

When we operate from the belief that resources are scarce, the game will always be rigged against us. And when we live in scarcity, exhausted and divided, we are prone to a disease of the mind, what I call the Consumer Condition. This is the belief there is only so much to go around, so everything is a win-lose transaction, rooted in competition, fear, destruction, and even entitlement.

We feel entitled when we are afraid.

consumer condition:

The belief that resources are limited so everything is a win-lose transaction rooted in competition, fear, destruction, and even entitlement.

Is it too late? Did I miss out? Am I capable? Will someone take too much and leave me without?

In scarcity, ownership by another means the loss of opportunity for oneself. Scarcity breeds fear, and that fear causes us to make irrational decisions (especially when it comes to our finances) that limit, rather than enhance, our life. In a world of potential freedom, joy, abundance, and service, a scarcity mindset allows us to see only limitations, suffering, poverty, and selfishness. It is crippling.

Scarcity is fueled by sacrifice.

Sacrificing who we are for what the world tells us to want.

Sacrifice misleads us. It tells us the only way to live the life we want is by doing things we hate, temporarily. What? To eventually have a better situation, we have to sacrifice our health, our time, and our quality of life so that one day, someday, we can finally be happy. But someday never comes. Someday doesn't exist.

We become our sacrifices.

It permeates all that we are and how we operate.

Sacrifice is the language of scarcity that convinces us we must do things we hate to provide a better life in the future and to live at the expense of enjoying things along the way. How can this be? Through the belief in scarcity. There is only so much time, limited money, or not enough ability.

Scarcity creates a long list of excuses disguised as evidence: why we aren't good enough, don't have enough, or don't deserve and should feel guilty about what we do have, and why limitation is something we simply must accept. The outcome is sacrifice—where we hear, accept, and then live by the myths and misinformation that hold us back.

Hustle, grind, and work.
I don't have the time.
I don't have the money.
I'll get to it later.
I'll be happy when_____.

SACRIFICE.

The list goes on and on. And that list controls our lives and shapes our futures.

That list also shapes our beliefs around how much money is enough. If we buy into it, we will remain stuck in the Consumer Condition; and no matter how hard we try, we will never find that magic number that will finally help us relax into life and find enjoyment in the abundance we've created.

If you've heard me speak or read my other books, you already know the cure for the Consumer Condition is to shift to what I call the Producer Paradigm. This is where you produce more value than you consume. Rather than focus on how much you can get (take) from the world, you create more *for* the world. Producers lift, bless, serve, and contribute. They operate in abundance, and their worldview includes expanded possibilities for value creation.

I had considered myself a producer, but now I was shaken because in the back

producer paradigm:

A worldview that emphasizes abundance, win-win interactions, service, stewardship, utilization, accountability, value exchange, and creation.

of my mind, the question lingered: What would I do with a billion dollars? I wasn't any closer to an answer. I still couldn't find the magic number that would unlock everything. And although I had started to free myself from the scarcity mindset, I still chased growth. I convinced myself that because I was contributing and creating value, then sacrificing family time, my health, and my own happiness for the business was okay—maybe even required.

Faulty philosophies learned at an early age, such as unprocessed feelings from being bullied or being told to suppress emotions, to not cry, or even mistakes, missteps, and difficult circumstances can all prevent us from finding contentment. These scenarios rob us from feeling abundant and loving our life, leading us to look for answers by pursuing money.

The pursuit of success or security through external validation (bank accounts, net worth, cars, houses, awards) leaves us either running or hiding from our past. We are rushing to fill the void, the holes, or prove something to someone else so we can feel whole. Or we may be hiding from the pain—from the beliefs and fears—to try and feel secure.

I kept trying to fill the holes with more. *More* success, *more* accolades, *more* money.

Until June 9, 2006.

The Worst Wake-Up Call

Thunderstorm warnings flash across the television and wake me up. I had fallen asleep on the couch in front of the TV. Tired and groggy, I turn off the TV and stagger to bed.

A few hours pass and I hear another unfamiliar sound. A ringing. My landline, which never rings, especially not this early in the morning. Not quite coherent, I ignore it. But then it starts ringing again and I pick up and blurt out, "WHAT?"

In a shaky voice, quiet and somber, my business partner Mike stumbles through a sentence or two before being able to articulate the devastating news. "No one has heard from Ray and Les since the plane left St. George last night."

I turn on the news in time to catch a breaking story.

A plane had crashed into Utah Lake.

Our plane.

Carrying three passengers. My partners Ray and Les, and Blaine, the pilot.

How could this be? Les wasn't initially scheduled to go but texted me last minute the day before, asking me to cover for him on our radio show. He wanted to support Ray and go have some fun in warmer weather.

My mind wanders to the partners meeting the week before where I expressed my concern about traveling too much and really wanted a break. Ray said he would love the opportunity to go in my place, so I gratefully let him take my seat on the plane.

In an instant, I snap out of it and immediately focus on how to help my partners' families. I rush to Ray's house. My mind races to thoughts of keeping everything together, our forty-two employees, three offices, a radio show, an event coming up, and . . . *Could this even be real?*

When I arrive at Ray's house, I have no idea how I got there.

That devastating wake-up call would lead to another wake-up call, one that would change the way I conducted every aspect of my life.

In the days, weeks, and even months after the plane crash, I coped by immersing myself even deeper in my work than ever before. I told myself that I had to work harder to preserve and protect my partners' legacies. The crash happened on a Thursday, and I was back in the office on Monday, even doing our two-hour radio show that morning. I started getting up even earlier to get to the office, which led to sleep deprivation.

I neglected my health. I gained weight. I didn't see my family much. My firstborn son had just turned one a few months before. He was asleep when I left for work in the morning and by the time I got home at night.

My first day off came four months later, at Thanksgiving. My wife, Carrie, and I drove a few hours to Price, Utah. Some of our best conversations happen on drives through the mountains, but on this trip, we were halfway through and had barely spoken a word.

Carrie broke the silence by saying, "Garrett, you're an extraordinary businessman, an extraordinary speaker, and an extraordinary radio show host." She then paused, glanced at our one-year-old son in the back seat, turned to me, and slowly spoke the words, "But you're just . . . an *ordinary* husband and father."

Initially, I looked away with embarrassment, choking back the tears. I swallowed, clenching my jaw to stave off the emotion. The feeling was overwhelming. I couldn't fight it off, ignore it, or push it down or away. The guilt and shame burst through—because she was right.

I figured hard work would make me successful. What it really made me was exhausted. Feeling frustrated and trapped, I had become disconnected from the most important people and aspects of my life.

I was supposed to be on that plane and yet was stuck in a

losing game with minimal reward or happiness due to my unexamined thinking and behavior. *You can't have it all*, I thought.

I was on this treadmill of sacrifice and hard work, running faster with no clear intention other than to keep things together and to make more.

There is that word again.

More.

An unattainable, ever-moving target that is misguided and that misleads us to sacrifice life—*our* life. The quest to obtain more had become my disease, and it led to disconnection and pain. All in the pursuit of more: More recognition. More clients. More status. I was chasing success with no room for fulfillment, but plenty of room for more pain.

When pain isn't addressed, it becomes addiction. For me that addiction was work. It is what I did, what I knew, but there is so much pain in what we think "we already know." I knew how to work hard and sacrifice at the expense of my happiness and my family. Worrying about others' feelings (customers, employees, peers) more than my own *or* my family, I had lost sight of the big picture.

Thanks to my wife's courage and honesty, everything changed—quickly. I let my employees know that I planned to take thirty days at home to focus on self-care and my family. I began working out again, playing with my son, and even found time to sleep and recharge.

Then something unexpected started to happen. Not only did I have renewed energy, but my income also started to rise as well. My entire mindset began to shift and transform as I invested in myself and emphasized quality of life.

In the two years prior to the plane crash, I had been tinkering with my first book. I had seventy-two choppy pages and a terrible title (*The Strongest String*). In the month I spent at home, I was able to finish the entire manuscript, all while spending more time with my family.

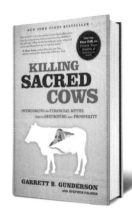

It was as if a portal to genius, a gateway of renewed energy, had opened up as my reward for removing busyness, being present, and investing time in what mattered most. That manuscript became the *New York Times* best seller, *Killing Sacred Cows*.

I put what had happened in a new context by creating a new narrative moving forward. I was learning from the past rather than being held captive by it—in essence, playing a new game. Instead of ruminating on the pain of the past, I chose to look at the pain as a gift.

I didn't love the packaging, of course. It created stress, sadness, and numbness; but that pain was my tap on the shoulder and kick in the ass to set me on a path of learning meaningful lessons, increasing gratitude, and finding purpose.

This pain became a driver for passion, a way to reconsider the direction I was heading and to determine what was most important—not the trappings of what society told me was important. One by one, I started dropping the myths by which I had lived my life. I abandoned the scarcity mindset and all the lies I had believed about money—for good.

And then, I asked myself a series of questions, which unlocked the hidden magic number. Those questions became the Value Index.

The Value Index

Now, right now, imagine you are given ten dollars every month, for the rest of your life, no strings attached. You don't have to come up with a way to get it. You don't have to work for it. You don't even have to ask for it. This is ten bucks above and beyond what you already have. Not a one-time extra ten; ten dollars free and clear, every single month, for the rest of your life.

What would you do with that extra money? Go to the movies? Save up for a bigger purchase? Pay down debt? Take a friend out for coffee?

How do you feel about having that money? Does the thought of getting an extra ten dollars every month matter? Does it make you feel excited? Hopeful? More secure?

Now, let's add a zero. Imagine you are given one hundred dollars every month, no strings attached, for the rest of your life.

What would you do? Would you invest the money? Spend it on date night? Hide it under your mattress for a rainy day?

How do you feel? Would this money make you feel happier?

Let's add another zero. Now you're up to one thousand dollars. Each and every month, for the rest of your life.

What would you do? Stop and think about it. Really ask yourself what you'd do with that money. There are so many options, right? Make a quick list.

How do you feel? Does the extra zero make a difference in your happiness? Does it make you feel better—less stressed, less worried, less scared? Does it make you feel hopeful?

Keep going. Add another zero. Imagine you receive, without any effort on your part and no obligation, ten thousand dollars every month for the rest of your life.

What would you do with it? How do you feel about it? Jot down your thoughts. I know you want to just keep reading, but remember, this is how we find that hidden number that works like a key to unlock you. So, play along. Take a minute, or half that, and really think about that ten grand showing up in your bank account like clockwork every month. What would you do, and how do you feel about that?

Okay. Let's go ahead and add another zero. You now get one hundred thousand dollars every month.

What would you do? Launch a new business? Build your dream home? Take time to travel the world?

How do you feel?

Relaxed?

Excited?

Overwhelmed?

Add another zero. You're up to one million now. Not once. Every. Single. Month. Yes, one million dollars every month. What would you do with that amount of money? Remember, you didn't have to earn it, find it, or ask for it. You don't owe anyone anything for it, and you don't have to pay taxes on it. How do you feel about being a millionaire every single month for the rest of your life?

Look at your answers at every stage. Quite different as the money increases. We're not done yet, but we're not going to add one zero. We're going to add two.

You know what's coming. Of course, I'm going to ask you the question that stumped me all those years ago, the question most people can't answer: What about a billion dollars? What if you were a billionaire?

If you can't come up with what you'd do with a billion dollars, don't spend too much time on it. It's not the point of this exercise, and it's not the hidden number.

This question, though—this is the question that matters:

At what point in this exercise did you stop thinking about what *you* could buy, or what the money could do for *you*, and start thinking about the value you could create for others? At what point did you create a vision rooted in value creation, focused on service?

What was your number?

If you made the flip at ten thousand a month, that is your hidden number. I call it the Value Index. This is the point when we turn our attention to value for others rather than consumption for ourselves. When we are in value creation mode, we are in service. We are focused on how we serve others, solve problems, and deliver value.

Ultimately, our vision isn't just about who we can create value for in the moment. It's really about what compels us to bring forth the best of who we are, the container in which we can add the most value.

soul purpose:

The combination of your passions, abilities, and values combined for the highest context of living. It is who you are when you are at your best, fully expressed.

Vision is the ultimate container in which to create value. It's what tells our brain what's important, what to pay attention to. The Value Index is simply where we are no longer worried about money, where we are no longer captive to the scarcity mindset and the win-lose zero-sum game of the Consumer Condition.

When you find your Value Index, when money is no longer your primary reason or excuse for doing or not doing something, the space for possibility opens up: "Maybe I'm here for something more. Maybe I can enjoy my life today. Maybe if I could really think about the best expression of my Soul Purpose, I could be free."

When we put value first, we can expand our vision. The Value Index is the number at which point we stop obsessing about how much we have so we can be the best of who we are.

It's Not about the Number

Now that you have your Value Index number, you may be thinking, "Now I have a goal to work toward." I get it. It makes sense. Why not work toward the number that will allow you to be of service?

Because the number doesn't matter. It's not about the number. It's about the perspective, the *vision*.

Vision is the ultimate container to create value. It creates context and determines actions. Now that you have your Value Index number, remove the constraints of time, money, and even ability. Those are only limiting factors when you try to do too much alone or too quickly. Just be willing to dream without restrictions. What calls to you? What compels you?

If money were of no concern, what would you do today? What have you been putting off? What have you been sacrificing?

This is your vision. Not the vision that is important to someone else, the one that calls to you. The one inside you, once you remember. Think back to the time before money determined your actions. Before stability and security crowded out your creativity. Or before you were driven by acknowledgment through awards, accolades, and financial accomplishments.

Your Value Index is about being in the mindset where it gets to be about you, your life, your vision today. Start thinking about how you can make that vision happen. Not *when* you get enough money to pull it off. But now—start *now*.

I know this may be hard to wrap your head around, but to truly change your financial destiny, you have to get to a mindset where money isn't a factor anymore, where it isn't your primary consideration for doing or not doing something. Then, create from that space.

You might be thinking, "Of course money is a consideration. We all need money." Yes, money is an essential tool. I mean, unless you want to live in the woods in a loincloth and shoot a bow and arrow. I tried that for five days and let me tell you, it was brutal. I took my kids to a survival camp. We lived in a teepee and had nothing except water and half of a saw. I thought it would be a blast, but it turned out to be something my friends would call "level two fun"—it's only fun or funny *after* it's over.

You've got bills. You may have kids to feed. I know you have to consider money. If it's wealth you want, though—if you want to truly build wealth—you have to get to the point where you use money and love people, not use people and love money. That's the difference. But you have to start with yourself.

Love yourself and build a life you don't want to retire from.

Most people go for the money first and create value second, but that's not going to get you out of the scarcity mindset. That's not going to help you build a life you love.

If your vision is powerful enough, it will create value. It will attract the right people. Your vision is the catalyst for you to create value. It informs your actions, demands attention, and directs focus, zeal, and energy. When you consider value first, when money is a by-product of

Mother Teresa of Calcutta

(1910–1997) was a Catholic nun known for her charitable work around the world. Her missionary work began in 1948 and within a year she founded a new religious community focused on serving the poor. By 2007, her community would grow to over 5,000 nuns and brothers, and hundreds of missions, schools, and shelters in 120 countries. Saint Teresa of Calcutta was canonized on September 4, 2016.

the value you create and is consistent with your quality of life, and your vision is worthy of your time and energy, you win. You are free.

A committed vision will attract opportunities for collaboration. And yes, it will attract money as well. It worked for me and for so many others you'll learn about in this book.

It also worked for Mother Teresa. People think she was poor, but she wasn't. Her vision was to help eradicate poverty, and she did—because money flowed to her like a river. She had enough money to change her corner of the world, to work toward a bold vision. Incidentally, she also flew on private planes. She never thought about money first, and as a result, she had enough of it to do the work she wanted to do. She didn't scrimp and save and hustle and grind to get the money so she could do that work *someday*. She didn't care about net worth or retirement plans. She worked toward her vision, and the money came to support it. Not through "the law of attraction" by merely thinking about it and wanting it, but by being in action and providing value.

Stop renting happiness. Expand your value. Focus on impact. Create a vision bigger than your problems. What speaks to you, inspires you? What would you dedicate your life to? One where your purpose is larger than any number in a retirement account.

Again, let me ask you: If money were of no concern, what would change in your life? What would you start doing? What would you stop doing? How would you show up differently?

You have your number now. And that number elicits a mindset that will help you unlock wealth, create purpose, move you from survival to service, and empower you to tap into your full potential.

In the coming pages, I'll show you how to free yourself from the money mindsets that have been holding you back, and how to use your number to change your financial destiny and build a life you love.

Win, Then Play

"People say nothing is impossible,
but I do nothing every day."

–WINNIE THE POOH

'm standing on a stage. The audience is quiet, waiting for me to begin. The crew is ready; they have eight cameras pointed at me. Months of daily rehearsals have led me to this moment. I've invested money, time, and called on favors. I've pushed myself to new levels of courage. I've done all I can. This is it. I have had the vision of walking through the curtains to the stage over and over. This is the moment it all comes together.

If I pull this performance off, I'll be on my way to the new life I envisioned. I'll even start to make money from this venture. I'll step into my new career. The "silly, ridiculous, impossible" dream to become a professional comedian will become real. We have eight Emmy winners on the crew and two roaming cameras capturing the audience with a packed house from the main floor to the balcony. This is the catalyst for television pitches, the upcoming multicity tour, and the new website that re-introduces me to my audience as not just a financial expert, but an entertainer with a bold mission to use humor to add love and laughter to one billion lives.

With these high stakes, you'd think I'd be racked with nerves. I should be concerned. The rehearsal the night before sucked. During the rehearsal, I was tired, stuck in my head, and I wasn't present, I wasn't having fun, and therefore the jokes didn't land well.

We only have this night to get it right, and at this point it's mostly on me. But I'm not nervous at all. I'm calm. I've let go of all the stakes, all my previous *mis*takes, and I'm here, present.

No thoughts of potential outcomes, I feel my breath, and my feet are planted firmly on these wooden boards.

I'm not worried at all.

I'm not worried because I've already won.

I won this game before I started playing it, before I wrote one joke.

I won this game first by designing *my* win, the process that mattered most to me, not to everyone else. What I want from this performance is to have fun, to be in flow, to enjoy the ride, and maybe even help my audience shift their perspective through laughter. I won when I laughed by myself as I wrote a joke. I won sharing it with my wife, my director, and my agent. I won each moment I was on a walk rehearsing or a comedy stage preparing, leading up to this night. It wasn't about someday or eventually. It wasn't just about that night or the outcome; the win is in the work. The rest—the footage, the gigs, the opportunities, the money, whatever comes next—all that is gravy.

I don't need these outcomes because my win is creative expression. Embracing the artist within me. Doing more of what I love. The stakes don't matter to me because they aren't *real* stakes. If the TV opportunities pan out, I'll be stoked, as long as I know my win and create the rules of what I'll do and not do. If I sell all my comedy tour tickets, that will be awesome. If I book a lot of theatrical keynotes, I'll be thrilled. But I'm not measuring the success of this comedy adventure by these outcomes. I'm not playing to win these outcomes, or playing to not lose these outcomes. Instead, the win is in the process, in the game I create.

I want to plant a seed of hope, connection, and expression

in the hearts of one billion people, and the way I do that is by doing everything I can to be an evolved human, to create a high quality of life for myself, to love myself, and to spend time with my family.

I've already won.

As the lights come up on me, alone on the stage, every cell in my body is alive with present-moment joy. I am in flow. Every thought that enters my mind is shared with my audience. Even the fact my son yawned in the crowd. I am present. Connected.

Despite all the perceived stakes, despite the Emmy-award winners on the crew or the cameras or the audience members, I won.

We live a world that defines our wins for us. Arbitrary net worth goals. Goal purchases. Goal weight. Goal rankings. Goals. Goals. Goals. We play by *other people's rules*, trying to either win the game, or not lose the game. Either way, we're doing life in sacrifice. Sacrificing who we are in the name of safety and security, time for money, all at the expense of today. But sacrifice is backward. The relentless pursuit of more, of eventually, of someone else's definition of a win, means we've already lost.

Rather than play to win, or play not to lose, we must Win, Then Play.

Playing to Win and Playing to Lose

Most of the world is stuck in scarcity, Playing Not to Lose. This is the place where people try to hold on to what they have, and hope nothing will ever change. A place that celebrates the cheap-skate or the miserable miser who lives to *save* rather than *serve*.

On the other hand, there are others who focus solely on the future as they hustle to compete and grab a bigger slice of the pie, while they exhaust themselves in the name of success. They are Playing to Win. And at what cost?

Playing to Win is a limited mindset. This may come as a surprise, especially since many entrepreneurs wear Play to Win as a badge of honor, a moniker. Those stuck in this mindset tend to take on too much risk and neglect other important areas of their life that aren't directly tied to money or accolades. They have no problem hustling and grinding, and they're most likely chasing the future. They often find worthiness in their net worth. This mindset rarely defines what a win looks like and crowds out room for enjoyment or quality of life along the way because it comes "at all costs."

Playing Not to Lose is a limited mindset as well. Those Playing Not to Lose hold on tightly to what they have and over-emphasize scrimping, rarely value their time, and hardly tap into their full ability to create value for others. Often they are stuck in the past doing everything they can to hold on to what they have. When people are trapped Playing Not to Lose, they hope nothing will ever change.

What is success, and what does success mean to you? Society will have us believe it is solely about recognition, money, and comparison: Do you have more than others? Again, society also tells us to sacrifice for "someday."

Win, Then Play isn't about someday. It is about now.

It's about creating a life you love and building a legacy that will last well beyond your lifetime. This isn't about retiring from a life you hate. It is about creating a purpose compelling enough to captivate you over a lifetime.

The odds are stacked against those who Play to Win and Play Not to Lose. The winners will be those of us who create a new game, a game worth winning—one where we maximize rewards with minimal risk by learning to win first, then play. Those who adapt, connect, and create value for others consistent with their purpose will own the future and enjoy the present. Money will be a by-product of creating value for and connecting with people.

Win, Then Play comes from focusing on your quality of life first and foremost; then your value is a by-product of a life well lived. And money follows value.

Win, Then Play is a mix of philosophy and practicality, and most importantly, a context to inform all choices going forward. When you Win, Then Play, you can flip focus on value creation over survival. You can create opportunity for others and yourself. Even if you think your resources (money, opportunities, time, connections) are limited, you can win.

win then play:

The philosophy and practicality of focusing on your quality of life first and foremost. Value is a by-product of your life well-lived. And money follows value.

I believe that true wealth, both material and non-material, comes from creating value consistent with a compelling purpose, meaningful moments, and having harmony in key areas of life: money, mindset, health, and recreation, securing prosperity while enjoying a life you love now. This is an entirely new model of life, business, and wealth creation.

Hard work and sacrifice sound great, until you give up who you are, what you are capable of, or what creates true joy. Win, Then Play teaches you how to define your win in a way that sets the context for your quality of life. Then, all your choices will support that goal. You won't be just another burnt-out employee chasing benefits while climbing the corporate ladder or an entrepreneur trapped in the hamster wheel of achievement. Neither of them stop to enjoy their lives and instead miss out on family time, all in hopes of a promotion or to avoid risking their legacy.

In the last chapter, I introduced you to the Consumer Condition, which emphasizes taking more than creating with win-lose transactions, and the Producer Paradigm, which emphasizes creating more than taking through win-win interactions. When we adopt the Producer Paradigm, we are fulfilled by living our Soul Purpose and helping others fulfill their objectives, in turn accomplishing our own. In this mindset, there is plenty of wealth to be created and to use. Our thoughts, emotions, and actions exist to contribute to our personal success and the success of others.

In Win, Then Play, we begin with value, expansion, and innovation, grounded in the belief that there are more than enough resources through human ingenuity. People who operate from abundance know that by creating value, and thus creating happiness in the lives of others, they bring more happiness to themselves. Instead of trying to exploit or dominate others in the struggle for limited resources, they can serve wholeheartedly and completely.

Define your game up front and make sure it is one worth winning. If you can't create a win *before* playing, you don't play.

Win, Then Play isn't about learning some tactic or strategy. It's about Soul Purpose, determining your game, and establishing the rules that serve you.

Vision is the win.

Value is the way.

Dollars are the by-product.

And prosperity is your state of being.

Start with a Hobby

By doing the Value Index exercise I had you try in the last chapter, I went from being stumped with the billion-dollar question to creating a vision of helping one billion people in the way I enjoy most: entertainment through performance and comedy. I don't worry about *not* seeing that vision come to fruition. That mindset would be Playing Not to Lose. I may not realize that vision directly, but we don't always know the ripples of our actions during our lifetime. And I don't worry about reaching one billion people before someone else does, or in a specific time frame, or if anyone will notice (and congratulate me) when I do. That mindset would be Playing to Win.

My Value Index vision is the container for my Soul Purpose. It can be as big as the sky. As big as the planet. As big as the galaxy. In fact, the bigger the better, because when we try to do seemingly impossible things, we find better, more impactful ways to do those things. Limiting the size of our container inevitably limits our imagination and the ability for others to support us as well.

I understand thinking about how to create a big vision may seem daunting. Where do you start? What are the steps? What is the right *first* step?

The right first step may surprise you.

Start with a hobby.

Yes, you read that right.

My in-laws used to say, "You have just two gears: first or turbo." I was either all-in working on something or doing nothing. After my wake-up call, I started thinking about being more intentional with my time. I thought about all the things I wanted to do that I never tried, because I couldn't see the payoff for my business. I used to think, Why would I pursue something if I couldn't make money from it? I set that mindset aside and took up all sorts of hobbies. I became a whiskey sommelier and a coffee barista. I started bow hunting and learned fly-fishing.

Often life can be difficult. There are a seemingly limitless number of problems and issues in the world that crowd out time to ourselves. These can become distractions and create dismay. Any personal issues we don't face up to, focusing instead on the things we wish were different, the pain we haven't resolved, or concerns we haven't processed—these can rob us of our time and energy.

This happens through escapism, which takes us out of flow. After I traded binge-watching sitcoms (or numbing out to sports talk programs, or debating politics) for hobbies, I was in flow. Hobbies eliminated the outside noise and helped me to find my inner voice, my vision. The pursuit of my interests *just because I wanted to* opened my mind and fed my soul. I started to see things differently. I enjoyed life more and I became happier.

And then I decided to seriously pursue a hobby I'd loved for a long time.

For as long as I can remember, I wanted to start and grow a successful business. But entrepreneurship wasn't my first love. My favorite hobby was comedy. One of my earliest memories is being with my family and laughing hysterically. Growing up, people would ask me, "Garrett, are you gonna tell us some jokes?" Comedy feels like love to me, like family. From the time I was five years old, I repeated jokes my dad and my uncles told me. Hearing my mom laugh is the best sound in the world.

As an adult, I told jokes to friends when out to dinner. I'd throw some into a keynote speech or a training. When I used comedy, people better understood the concepts I taught. They got it. They remembered. They learned. Comedy is how I prefer to go through life.

One of my big goals in life was trying to get my wife, Carrie, to laugh. Most of the time, she didn't. I kept working on it. Then one day I told her some jokes at an event, and she said, "That was funny."

Days later I was giving a speech and the host introduced me as hilarious. Oh, I was about to give a financial talk and he called me hilarious. What? So, I told a few jokes, got some laughs, and within hours of walking off stage I scheduled an open mic.

I called my friend Marcus, a comedian, to help me out, and within a week, I did my first four-minute-and-twenty-second set. I was hooked. I started opening for the *Marcus and Guy Show*, and two years later to the day, I was approached by an agent. Then, on April 15, 2021, I recorded my first comedy special.

Despite all these milestones, comedy was still my hobby. I did it for the sheer joy of it, for the pursuit of artistic excellence, for the unfolding of a dream.

I started to connect the dots between my Value Index vision to help a billion people and my comedy hobby. What if I could get there faster by sharing my knowledge in a humorous way? What if I could realize my vision and have the best time doing it? Pursuing my hobby, which from the outside looking in could be seen as a time and money suck, actually helped me see a way forward. After comedy shows, people came up to talk to me about how my messages hit home with them. That never happened after my old keynotes. When I realized people are more likely to have a transformative experience when they laugh, my vision materialized.

> We get so fixated on the "hows" of life,
> and yet it's the "loves" that make things happen.

The things we love to do. The people we love to spend time with. The interests we love to learn more about. That's the way forward. It nourishes our soul, energizes our life, and opens up our ability to articulate and discover our vision.

I have other hobbies (shooting my bow, fly-fishing, latte art) that may never make me a dime or may even cost me money, but it is in taking time for self-care, enjoying life along the way, that we find our voice, our purpose. When our life is defined by money, we lose. When there is no room for what we enjoy, we lose touch with our intuition and are unable to determine our path.

It can be hard to come up with your win before you play. You've been told by well-intentioned preachers, teachers, family, and friends what to do, how to do it, what success is, and what it isn't. To unwind all that messaging, find something that is just for you. Something that has no money in it. Something you enjoy for "no good reason." Start with a hobby and you'll find yourself.

The Validation Trap

It's easy to get trapped living someone else's vision for us, especially when we think we must earn their love or acceptance, or that having more or accomplishing something will help us love ourselves more.

Instead, be willing to listen to your intuition, quiet and soft, but strong. You may not feel prepared for the answer or know what to do in the moment, but all you have to do is take one step. That step being, **speak it into existence**. Yes, speak your vision into existence for no other reason than you were bold enough to consider it.

It takes a leap of faith in yourself to say a vision out loud that you don't have all the answers for or the details of how to accomplish. If we don't know what to do with a billion dollars, it is a vision problem. If we are taking our money and handing it over to investments we can't relate to before investing in our skill sets, into our hobbies, or into our quality of life, we sacrifice. We lose.

If we aren't sure what to do with our money, it isn't from a lack of quality investments, it's from a lack of vision. Often it's easier to allocate money toward something when we have no control over the outcome (like a stock) or any relationship to the value, simply because everyone else is doing it. But investing in outside things before investing in yourself, or investing in your vision, will not and cannot lead to your win. It is a delay, a detour to your winning game.

When you focus on a vision that is compelling to you, rather than validation from others, you win. Self-responsibility means we don't listen to the critics for the win. We are responsible for our vision, but not for others' opinions. The Consumer Condition may run in the background and ask: What if I don't know how to do it? What if it hasn't been done before? What if my truth causes controversy? Recognize most people stuck in the Consumer Condition will have an opinion that won't serve you.

Because so few people are playing a game worth winning (and most people are stuck in the Consumer Condition), vision is discounted and dismissed, tossed aside as something childish. Once celebrated as cute, now criticized as impossible, the Consumer Condition will say, "Grow up and get in reality." Oh right, the real world—that place filled with fear, doubt, worry. The place with all the knowledge of why something can't work, won't work, and with hardly any energy left to create what will.

It is important to understand where these intellectual and articulate doubters are coming from. They see your Soul Purpose as impossible, because only you can speak the language of your

Soul Purpose. They don't know how to decipher the symbols and characters of it, because it doesn't exist in that exact form inside anyone else. And it won't exist in the world unless you unleash it, unlock it, and reveal it through creation and value.

People fear what they don't understand, reject what they can't comprehend, and protect what they are already committed to: the losing games. When people are committed to the losing games, they defend their actions. They don't want to think all the sacrifice was leading them to a place of limitation, erroneously believing it was a requirement for success.

In losing games, we get attached to being right or not being wrong. It is human nature.

The best way to escape the trap is to embrace possibility, to speak your vision in a language that everyone can understand even if they fear it. It won't be exact the first time you say it; it needs time to grow and evolve. Vision is more of a lab than an equation. It will course correct along the way. But the losing games force us to make changes that are costlier and more painful. The vision muscle grows stronger with use, and with practice.

Create Your Future

President Abraham Lincoln once said, "The best way to predict the future is to create it." Regardless of our past, we choose our next step, thus creating our future story. We can rewrite the ending as the value creator, rather than as the victim. We can embody a story where we enjoy the moments along the way and appreciate the space in between—a story in which we find the most meaningful ways to create value.

I had believed that life and success were about sacrifice. That if I wanted to win, it was about being willing to outhustle and grind it out to eventually get where I wanted to go. I was misinformed and misled.

The game of more is unwinnable.

I had been focused on quantity of stuff and external validation, stuck on a philosophy that crowded out meaningful moments, relaxation, rejuvenation, or any form of recreation. I had all the appearances of material wealth and plenty of accolades, but I was miserable and causing damage to those I love. I didn't have the conscious intention to create a life I truly wanted.

To heal from a losing game, we first have to know we're playing it. Most of the time, we don't have a clue.

In the next chapter, I'll help you discover the traps that create losing games. Without this awareness, executing your Value Index vision will be a major challenge, if not impossible. It's time to shrug sacrifice, discover the trappings of scarcity, and instead create a game worth winning.

The Losing Games

"Life moves pretty fast. If you don't stop and look around every once in a while, you could miss it!"

—FERRIS BUELLER,
Ferris Bueller's Day Off

"We've only sold half the venue," Barry told me. "You need to get on it and sell more tickets."

It was the day after Thanksgiving, with the last show in Philly coming up in three days. I had been in fifteen different cities for my comedy tour. I was exhausted and annoyed. Despite being an unknown comic, I'd sold out twelve of the fifteen venues. But Barry wanted a completely sold-out tour to impress the club owner and TV executives he planned to pitch. I'd bought into this thinking and spent countless hours calling in favors to get tickets sold. I'd lost sleep over delays on the ticketing page of my new website and created a rift with my business partner. I'd also missed important time with my wife, who had to unpack the boxes from a move without me.

Hearing the frustration in Barry's voice, it suddenly dawned on me that I had lost my win. In the absence of my clarity, he offered up suggestions. And to please him, I'd bought into *his* win. The fifteen-city tour wasn't my vision; it was his. If I had thought about it, if I had considered how the tour would impact my life and how to make it a win for me before I agreed, I would have pushed the tour back a year. But I had been riding high on the success of the comedy special, and that created a sense of urgency, well, even scarcity in me.

Scarcity took over. It went a little something like this: I've got to do this tour to get the special sold to Netflix.

Netflix.

Then I would be a real comedian. Then I would be known, accepted, and validated. Netflix was my game, my trophy. I was striving, I was Playing to Win. Damn it, I should know better. I'm writing the book on this. Progress, not perfection.

Somehow Netflix was going to define success for me.

Why?

To feel cool because I was on the app, on TV, and this would prove to people who ever doubted me they were wrong? Or because I somehow felt, or heard, Netflix meant comedians "made" it? This goal was for someone else's approval or acceptance, because I got caught in the trap. The trap of *if, then, when*. *If* I get Netflix, *then* I'll be happy. *When* people see (and like) the special, that is. So many conditions for my happiness and life were now outside my control. Ultimately, this wasn't a win because it minimized my love and my passion for comedy; it reduced it to a future fleeting moment, a goal. Goals can be great, unless the joy in the process is lost, or it becomes more about sacrifice rather than art, play, or value.

That's the danger of success—suddenly you forget your own rules, your values, and what got you there in the first place. That was the trap. Playing someone else's game, no matter the reason.

When my partners died in the plane crash, I worked harder than ever because I wanted to preserve their legacy. But it came at the expense of mine, at the cost of my quality of life. I did it because I thought it was noble, because I thought it was the right thing to do, but at what cost? And here I was, chasing happiness through Netflix, caught in another losing game.

"I gave my word to the owner that we would sell out," Barry continued. He didn't believe we could do it.

The smart-ass in me replied, "Then he shouldn't be disappointed. He was right."

Here's the thing. *I* didn't give my word to the owner we'd sell out the venue. Plus, I didn't even give my word to *Barry* that we'd sell out. But somehow, I forgot that and took on his win as my own. Look, this wasn't even his fault. I love Barry. He wants me to win, but how can he help me or how can I win, when *I* didn't know my win?

Success, drama, or trauma can trigger old patterns. In these scenarios, scarcity grips us and a Shadow Persona can take over. We all have them, and they keep us stuck in the losing games.

The Four Shadow Personas

In my theatrical keynote, *Already Won*, I perform a scene from an imaginary road trip. On this trip there are four passengers. If you found yourself on this imaginary road trip, within ten minutes you'd probably jump out the imaginary door of the imaginary moving car and drop-and-roll yourself to freedom. Because these people are *a lot to handle*. They represent the Four Shadow Personas that drive most of us:

These Four Shadow Personas evolve from the Consumer Condition and are reinforced by our inherited money mindsets and unresolved childhood pain and trauma. Fun times, right? We typically let one of the

shadow personas:

Four personas evolving from the Consumer Condition and reinforced by our inhered money mindsets and unresolved childhood trauma

The personas are:

- The Striver
- The Miser
- The Conservative
- The High Roller

The Striver

The Miser

The High Roller

The Conservative

personas drive us at any given time, though sometimes one of them is a back seat driver.

Now that you have your Value Index number, the next step is to become aware of the Shadow Persona that may be driving your financial, business, and life decisions. Because if anything can derail the pursuit of your vision, it's these assholes. Once you gain that awareness, you can flip to your Winning Persona.

In my keynote, the four passengers in the car are annoying. They argue with each other. They can't work together. They are focused only on their own goals, not the ultimate goal: getting to their destination. In *your life*, the four passengers—our Shadow Personas—keep us from enjoying the ride, from noticing the scenery, from having great experiences with the people we care about, and from meeting interesting people along the way, people who could help us get where we're going. They might even prevent us from ever arriving at our destination.

We may let one persona drive for most of our life, but most of us switch off with at least one more from time to time. It's rare to let all four Shadow Personas have a chance to drive our life and work, but we certainly allow other people in our lives to make decisions for us using *their* personas.

The Striver

Strivers play the status game. They are all about making it big—and being seen for it. They feel distracted when you're around them. At times you may not feel important to them because they are busy earning and doing, and you might be getting in their way. They are natural competitors who yearn to reach the top of the mountain of success. Expect the Striver to outwork anyone or at least try at all costs: health, family, hobbies. There is never enough as they conquer and accumulate.

When I started playing Barry's game during my comedy tour, it's this persona that I fell back into without even realizing it.

What do Strivers do for enjoyment? Work.

What is their idea of a social life? Networking.

What do they think is a good meal? Either the very best or else it better be fast.

Money matters because they believe it gives them status. They love credentials, titles, or some version of corner offices, flashy watches, and cars. They often use the language of revenue to brag about their accomplishments. They talk a big game, but their daily life likely tells a different story. The Striver is unpleasable.

Because they tend to place more value on how they are

perceived than on how they live, Strivers often work long, hard hours. They need bigger, better, faster. They climb the ladder, and everyone looks up to them as "successful." But if anyone saw a Striver's personal life, few would envy them. They sacrifice relationships in the pursuit of status and prestige. One day, when they reach the top, they finally realize they are lonely and unsatisfied. That status comes at the cost of real enjoyment in life. Too late, they see that what matters isn't what you make, but what you keep, how well you use it, and your quality of life.

This was almost my story. Until I got my wake-up call.

Chris Zaino was stuck in this game when I met him in 2012. According to most, he was winning at life. He ran the largest-volume chiropractic office per square foot in history. He was considering building new offices.

Unfortunately, he had no time for anything but work. He was no longer sure what winning meant. His body was breaking down. Hobbies he once loved, and in which he excelled, had been crowded out of his life. Scarcity ran the show. In the back of his mind, it whispered, "Go for more. Do more. Work harder." It became all he knew.

Then I asked him, "What do you really want?" Chris had to do some soul searching to see that he needed space. He wanted to enter bodybuilding competitions, play piano again, and create memorable experiences with his sons. But his constant striving had left him no room for these things.

As a Striver, it seemed from the outside that Chris had it all. But even after checking all the boxes society told him mattered, he felt empty on the inside. He nearly lost everything that mattered: his health and his joy.

The Miser

Misers play the hoarding game. They are the most fearful of the four Shadow Personas. They hate spending and value frugality above all. They are penny pinchers who believe in holding on to as much of their earnings as they can. They are control freaks because they don't trust anyone with their money. They typically focus on ways to spend less, save more, and put every possible penny into low-risk, low-reward vehicles like savings accounts, CDs, money market accounts, savings bonds, or in the case of some of my family: coffee cans.

Expect Misers to save at all costs by coupon clipping, cutting back, or living off rice and beans.

DISCOUNT 30%

My wife, Carrie, and my family had to deal with my being a Miser early in my life. Like many budget-minded people, I used to obsess over expenses. I didn't consider quality of life. I was all about saving. If Carrie wanted to get a drink with dinner, I'd say, "Just get the water, then we can put more money in savings."

We'd get into fights about my cheapskate attitude and my inability to enjoy the life I had in favor of a life I thought I was planning for.

Once, before our second child was born, I took my family to San Diego for a vacation. We visited some parks and saw some sights, but that was about it. I packed a bag that we carried on the flight. I brought along food, so no dining out—not even drinks—and even tried to get us to skip meals or eat canned food at the hotel. If we did go anywhere, our flights were extended layovers or red-eyes because it saved money.

Instead of enjoying my family and sharing new experiences, I focused on tabulating every dollar and cent. I worried every moment that I wasn't at work making money. I constantly studied bills to see what we could eliminate or reduce. This led to one of the biggest fights my wife and I had early in our marriage. I would go through our budget and consistently berate her about any money she spent as a teacher to improve her classroom or invest in her students. I would say things like, "You are supposed to get paid *for*, not *pay* for, teaching." She later admitted that our first year of marriage was the hardest because she felt minimal freedom and was afraid to spend money because it might upset me. Wow.

In 2005, I met an engineer, Dale Clarke, at a workshop I was teaching. He was an even bigger Miser than I had been. Dale was obsessed with budgeting. He believed that if he saved like no one else, he could one day live like no one else. When he was a child, his family lived off peanut butter and Miracle Whip sandwiches because jam was a luxury. During his early married life, he and his wife shopped for birthday and Christmas presents for their kids at Goodwill, spending cents, not dollars, and being obsessed about holding on to more and more money. They were both Misers because they had the attitude it might lead to becoming millionaires—at least on paper, though they'd go on living like paupers. By letting a budget dictate their mindset, by letting constraint govern personal and financial decisions, they were delaying enjoyment—and the joy of life.

The ultimate reward of the preservation game is to save money, but never enjoy it.

The Conservative

Conservatives play the accumulation game. To be clear, "Conservative" has nothing to do with a political position. It is a paradigm, a Shadow Persona. They may have similar fears as the Miser, but they are a bit more conscientious. They are diligent long-term investors and wonderful savers who consider themselves wise with money. Conservatives believe slow and steady wins the race. You'll often hear them say, "I'm in it for the long haul." They tend to use traditional financial vehicles like 401(k)s, IRAs, index funds, and the like.

A Conservative's primary financial goal is to save enough money to retire. They are saving for "someday," which often never comes. And they miss out on joy and opportunities because they won't veer off their "long haul" plan. Unfortunately, because of the vehicles and strategies they use, their retirement funds typically have limited access, that is unless they are willing to pay penalties (which they are most definitely not). Conservatives can't spend down the principal for fear of running out of money before they die. Yet they face steep tax penalties when using these funds. Furthermore, in retirement plans, their

money is subject to market volatility. Like so many risk-averse people, Conservatives are exposed to substantial risk without realizing it. They may learn, to their horror, that retirement funds can plummet overnight in market downturns due to pandemics, recessions, and flash crashes. Expect them to blame others or the stock market for their circumstances.

Brian Baird described himself as "old school conservative" when we first met just after the global financial crisis in 2008–2009. At fifty-seven years old, he'd had a twenty-plus-year career at a large company and a nice nest egg in his 401(k). Then he realized how quickly it could all disappear. What was the point of being a dedicated scrimper-saver, and eternally deferring his enjoyment, when it could all get cut in half with factors outside of his influence or control?

He felt that something was missing, or that there was more he could or should be doing. But he couldn't see what that was. His conservative viewpoint had him focused on reduction rather than production, and on delaying gratification at all costs.

The Conservative works hard in the hope of large rewards in the distant future, but loses by missing out on the now.

The High Roller

High Rollers play the opportunity game. They constantly scan the horizon for the "next big thing." You name it, they've tried it all—real estate, network marketing, day trading, buying cryptocurrency, whatever. They follow all the hot trends and tend to invest from greed. Thus, they often buy high and sell low because they are reactionary, not strategic. Unlike Conservatives, they don't have the patience to wait for thirty years to get wealthy—they're looking for fast riches. They are quickly bored and rarely stick with anything long enough for it to pay off. If High Rollers ever do make it big, it's usually after a few monumental failures.

Expect High Rollers to be great entertainers, if you can handle the inauthentic nature of their stories, their braggadocio, and their constant one-upmanship.

My shortest but most expensive stint as a High Roller came a few years into my twenties. I had started to see some success in my business and met a group of High Roller entrepreneurs. They were into real estate deals, fancy cars, and private planes. Hanging with them caused my greed gland to grow—as did my risk. I had the High Roller's belief that looking wealthy would attract more wealth and business,  but in several circles, it created doubt, and for good reason. During this time, the economy was robust and interest rates were low, so people were able to buy nicer homes than they could afford and to finance exotic cars. They had wonderful—borrowed—lifestyles. And it wasn't sustainable, or as wonderful as it appeared.

Playing the High Roller's game changed me for a while, and not for the better. I still cringe when I remember the time a magazine interviewed me for a cover article on success in my newly finished, award-winning commercial building filled with objects that demonstrated wealth, but really were a way to burn money. It's embarrassing to admit, but I told the interviewer how I had "so much real estate kicking off cash flow" and had "so much money, I wouldn't be able to spend it all." That wasn't even my worst moment.

At one event, when the valet didn't park my Bentley up front, I turned to my wife and said, "What's wrong with him?"

"What's wrong with *you*?" she promptly replied.

Then the economy quickly corrected my arrogant and ignorant ways.

At the time, I was invested in more than one hundred real estate properties that I wasn't properly managing and had created a hard money lending fund (doing short-term, high-interest-rate loans, financing real estate projects); plus, I was in oil and gas investments and more. I chased opportunities, blind to the risk. I wasn't doing this because of a vision aligned with my Soul Purpose. I had confused luck and timing with skill and ability, and because at the time, my self-worth was tied to my net worth.

When the dust settled, I lost—and lost big. This took a decade to fully recover from as I chose to pay with my time because, for me, bankruptcy wasn't an option. I attempted to make investors whole; however, some wouldn't even talk to me. I thought I was being financially savvy, but it led to neglect. Neglect of my family and my quality of life. I was always on the phone, or on a computer, or at an event working on investment deals.

This created the most stress and damage for my marriage, my family, and some of those who handed me their money. It took me hundreds of hours to communicate with and repair relationships, to restore integrity, and it cost me millions of dollars to pay back investors. With High Rollers using their appearance of wealth as the main way to attract clients and investors, it can come crashing down quickly when things don't go well.

I did learn some of the most valuable lessons of my life, though.

I'll highlight a few signs to watch for so you can avoid the mistakes that come along with this Shadow Persona.

First, High Rollers love to ask questions that are merely set-ups for them to brag. They aren't interested in your answer; they want to give you theirs. Second, they are likely to exaggerate and name drop. Third, they always have a deal or something they can offer for you to be involved in. They aren't likely to use their money, especially if they can get you to part with yours.

There is an art to the High Roller. Some may seem subtle, but they find a way to let you know how important they are; yet others are the life of the party. Some of the most publicized scandals come from High Rollers: Bernie Madoff. Jordan Belfort (*The Wolf of Wall Street*). Elizabeth Holmes.

High Rollers cut corners, take substantial risks, and are likely to go bankrupt—and lose other people's money along the way.

The Winning Personas

Far too many people get sucked into Shadow Personas because they don't look down the road to see what will happen if they "win" their chosen game. The Miser ends up with cash he won't spend. The Conservative ends up with retirement funds he *can't* spend for fear of running out. The Striver burns out. The High Roller winds up with short-lived riches.

The Shadow Personas are selfish, trapping us in a losing game. We may not be one of these Shadow Personas all the time, but we aren't so enlightened that none of these personas show up in our lives from time to time.

Sometimes aspects of these personas can be useful to us. Being thrifty isn't a bad thing. Neither is saving money. But when we limit joy, and the happiness of those we love, that's a *losing* game.

Working hard is noble and yields rewards. But when we push so hard that we push others away, or we ignore our own health, or our family, *that's* also a losing game. And willingness to take chances can help you achieve your goals. But when we do this and put our family at risk, requiring way more time and money than we promised, we compromise our integrity. We lose, and so do the people who care about us the most.

Perspective determines our responses, reactions, and beliefs. Simply seeing things from a scarcity mindset can destroy happiness, reduce value exchange, and limit results. The same abilities, characteristics, and passions can become a Winning Persona with a different paradigm, new rules, and a better game.

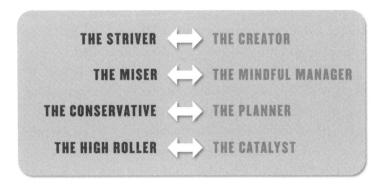

A Winning Persona is unlocked when your focus becomes about value, service, and solving problems for others. It is the shift from me to we, from a limited game to an expansive game.

The Striver is an impatient, busy malcontent. However, on the flip side is their Winning Persona, the Creator, an innovator or entrepreneur. They create with ingenuity and invention, which brings opportunity for others, as it takes a team to implement their vison. The Creator focuses on self-discovery to find contentment in the value they create, unveiling their inner artist.

Chris Zaino was able to flip to his Winning Persona, finding new, healthier ways to produce that connected to his true passions. He started an online program where other doctors could see how to run an efficient business, give health talks to potential patients, and see all the processes that were built to handle such a large volume of patients. He found ways to create new income without wearing down his body. He embraced improving his industry and building something that hadn't existed before, creating new jobs, and expanding his value. This allowed him to go on meaningful trips with his kids, something he only did once in the previous seven years. Now he plans time off for a trip at least monthly *and* is able to create enough value to keep increasing his income, without sacrificing his quality of life.

The Miser is a judgmental, pessimistic cheapskate. Yet, the Miser's Winning Persona is the Mindful Manager—detail-oriented, efficient, and great at improving things. This persona is instrumental for any organization looking to be more resourceful, to reduce waste, and to be more efficient.

As a Miser, Dale Clarke obsessed about how he could save money by cutting back and cutting out. His Winning Persona leveraged his attention to detail in outlining a process called cash flow optimization, which resulted in thousands of people keeping more of what they earned. He helped them shave off one-third or more of the time it took to pay off loans and revolutionized the way they understood money.

As an engineer, Dale had always had the ability to create a system and see critical pieces missed by most people, but in his

Shadow Persona, he limited the benefits of this talent to budgeting and cutting back instead of creating value for others. Following what he learned at Wealth Factory, Dale created economic independence in 362 days and moved from survival to value for others. Now Dale makes ten times more income. He lives in his dream home, takes vacations, and invests money on things to add value to others, which led to his increased income and impact. This allows Dale to enjoy life along the way, and he is now a great gift giver, something that he was blinded to in his Shadow Persona.

The Conservative is a hesitant, overly analytical know-it-all. On the flip side, their Winning Persona is the Planner, a stable, secure, thoughtful, and strategic person, who can be instrumental in minimizing risk, planning for contingencies, and monitoring the effectiveness of any initiative.

Brian Baird flipped to his Winning Persona, which freed him from an obsession about retirement planning to an ability to create cash flow; this allowed him to finally see himself and his ability to serve others as his greatest assets. Brian moved from the scarcity-based "someday" mindset of the Conservative, to the add-more-value now and in the future nature of the Planner. His greatest revelation: "Through your own abilities you can actually create more worth—financially and otherwise—for yourself using your own talents now!"

The High Roller can seem narcissistic at times as a one-upping name-dropper. On the flip side is the Winning Persona—the Catalyst: a visionary and a connector. They think and play big, and uplift others by finding ways to grow together. They see investments as relationships and ways to create value.

High Rollers take from one's vision, while Catalysts co-create it. Catalysts are instrumental in bringing a vision to life. They grow businesses, connect us to fascinating people, and without them, this book wouldn't be possible because of the opportunities, connections, and encouragement the Catalysts in my own life have provided.

After I hung up my High Roller ways, I kept the best aspects of that persona: the co-creation. Since then, I've dedicated my life to focusing on working with others to bring my vision to life and connecting others with the people who can help them do the same.

You may already have a sense of which Shadow Personas you've allowed to drive your life and work. It's not a great feeling, realizing you've not only been holding yourself back, but you've also been making yourself miserable and possibly hurting people you love. Remember, our Shadow Personas are created by our unprocessed pain, childhood trauma, and the scarcity mindset. You didn't consciously choose to limit yourself or others in these ways. You see the truth now, and you'll do better. You'll start to let a Winning Persona drive instead.

After my conversation with Barry about selling out the comedy venue, I realized I'd fallen back into my Striver ways. That awareness is all it took to let go of that side of me immediately and flip into Creator mode. That night in Philadelphia, I focused on giving value to my audience. Several collaborators had made the trip for the show that night, and I expressed my gratitude and love for them. It was a fantastic night and a win for me because I decided in advance that my win would not be measured by ticket sales; it would be measured by giving value, expressing gratitude, and having fun.

Flipping from the Shadow Persona to the Winning Persona is about expanding your value. It's not just about how much money you have, but how well that money serves you in terms of living a life you love, and how it serves others. In chapter 1, you discovered your Value Index. When you find yourself behaving like or thinking like one of your Shadow Personas, a quick way to snap out of it and connect back to your Soul Purpose is to revisit your Value Index number.

To give your Winning Personas "the wheel," to *bring them forth*, initiate the four-step process I share in the next chapter, The Flip.

The Flip

"Clear eyes, full hearts can't lose."

–COACH TAYLOR,
Friday Night Lights

Gravity

t's 2008. The economy is crashing. I'm speaking at an event, and I'm talking about Soul Purpose. I explain that it is your values, passions, and abilities combined for the highest context of living. As defined in chapter 1, Soul Purpose is who you are when you are at your best. The highest levels of joy and fulfillment come from knowing and living within it.

From the stage, I notice a six-foot-seven-inch giant man with tears rolling down his cheeks.

After I finish speaking, he approaches me and tells me his name is Brad and he's from Garland, Texas.

"I'm ready to shut it all down," he says. "If I sell my dental practice in Garland, I can pay off my debt. I have barely enough money in the bank to live on. But if I move to a one-bedroom apartment and drastically cut expenses . . ."

Brad was exhausted and broke. Tired of being in debt. Tired of always worrying. He had been simply practicing dentistry, with no rhyme, purpose, or reason beyond survival, which he was barely able to hang on to, considering he wasn't even able to afford dental supplies.

He felt old.

The losing game of the Consumer Condition had him trapped.

Brad had recently met Carolyn, but he couldn't afford an engagement ring, so he had to use her credit card to buy one.

When he took Carolyn to meet with his accountant, he slipped out to use the bathroom. His accountant advised her not to marry him, at least not until his $150k IRS debt was handled. Carolyn felt the situation was so desperate, her Shadow Persona, the Miser, created a list of things to do if they were going to get married: budget, scrimp, and cut way back. Sacrifice. Brad, the Striver, felt conflicted, even tortured, as it seemed like an unwinnable situation—love or freedom—and he didn't know what to do.

The situation and the dueling Shadow Personas delayed their wedding, and the world, wondering why the engagement was so long, assumed it was Brad holding back.

Brad stopped dreaming because he felt his life was now all about survival, which is a selfish state of mind that repels wealth. Reductionist thinking removes possibility. What can be reduced, eliminated, or done less expensively doesn't take into consideration how you can impact the people you serve the most, or to invest in yourself and bring out the best there is to offer.

When I spoke of Soul Purpose, it struck a chord for Brad, which brought him to tears. It was the escape plan from his mental prison, a place where he could have it all. It was all about adding value. It was about living purpose. It was about investing in himself. It was about expanding his means to live within them. It was about embracing his Winning Persona, the Creator.

He'd always had the tools to be a value creator, but they were buried in his Shadow Persona. In a moment, there was a flip, a new focus. He had permission to dream again. He now had the awareness that he'd been living in scarcity, and he started to create a new vision.

Brad added more value to existing patients by creating new skill sets to solve sleep apnea, detect cancer, and collaborate with other doctors. He took those funds and reinvested them into a beautiful practice. Carolyn leveraged her Mindful Manager persona to build systems. She moved the practice from a small office in a 1950s house to a new building that looked like a beautiful hotel lobby.

No longer focused on shutting down his practice, Brad started to focus on collaboration. He found a niche that he was uniquely gifted to support: older dentists who weren't busy enough to bring in an associate and who were stuck in a situation like the one he had faced. These doctors didn't have the knowledge or energy to grow their practice or hire associates as they grew fatigued. If they sold their practice, there wasn't enough to live on—that is, unless they moved to a one-bedroom apartment with a plastic box chair.

Brad began to co-create with Wealth Factory (and a consulting company called Next Level Practice) and came up with a model for these baby boomer dentists.

Brad now has entirely new conversations. He talks about how he can continue to improve the dental profession, and how he can pay his success forward.

At age sixty-four, Brad's once-crumbling life is now fresh, exciting, and fulfilling. He brings in seven figures, nearly four times what he earned in his best years. He has helped countless dentists grow their practices, and he recently purchased his ninth location.

More offices didn't mean more time at the office. Brad recently bought a new boat and paid cash. Most evenings you can find Brad heading to CC dock, his own slice of heaven, a boating dock with a fridge, grill, and all the necessities to get relaxed before going out on his boat. Brad was enjoying the fruits of his labor and wasn't relegated to a small apartment, but instead has a beautiful home, additional properties, and horses.

4 STEPS TO A WINNING GAME

1. CO-CREATE

2. ELIMINATE

3. DELEGATE

4. COLLABORATE

Brad told me, "Life has never been this good. I have to pinch myself, it is just crazy."

Oh, and he turned down a multimillion-dollar buyout, because he has purpose, and that is something money can't buy.

Your Value Index vision is the ultimate container in which to focus, create value, and leverage your Winning Persona. Yet we can lose sight of it if we stay wrapped up in our Shadow Personas. To leave a losing game and flip to a game worth winning, there are four key steps.

Step One: Co-Create

When people think they must do everything by themselves, they get trapped in a Shadow Persona. Find one other person with whom you can share your ideas or issues, someone who can support or inspire you. Find a co-creator who can create accountability or possibility to move beyond the Consumer Condition and into creation.

Every book I've written has been a co-creation, even with co-authors. Even when I don't have co-authors, I have an amazing editing team. I feel that sometimes my editor is a co-author, because her questions are brilliant, and she talks about how we're going to organize the book. She also gives me the reassurance that *done* is better than *perfect*, because I know that editors are going to clean up the manuscript, so it doesn't have to be flawless the first time around.

My wife is the ultimate co-creator (there is a joke in there, I know, as we have two kids). When I'm in a moment of doubt or frustration, she helps me to think about things that wouldn't occur to me otherwise. When I want to blame someone else, she says, "I wonder what the other person's perspective is."

Co-creators can help cultivate ideas and offer support. They can use a questioning process to bring out information.

When I do stand-up comedy, it's a co-creation process at the open mic, telling a joke and finding out whether the crowd laughs or not.

When people are in isolation and hit a level of frustration so that it doesn't feel like a game anymore, it's because they're doing too much alone. Co-creation is instrumental, not only in accelerated results but in enjoyable results.

Step Two: Eliminate

Before you start something new, create space for your life and let something go. I have a simple philosophy: if I buy new clothes, I have to give something away. If I buy a new shirt, I give a shirt away. It just so happens that my dad and I are a similar size, so he has a great wardrobe, because I like to get new clothes. Sometimes if my clothes shrink, I give them to my brother-in-law, Bobby, because he's a little smaller than I am.

Elimination is simple from a physical standpoint, but it can be more difficult to eliminate escapisms—the issues that you are putting off or sweeping under the rug, hoping they go away, things you are hiding or running from and don't want to address. Escapisms show up in the form of distractions, detours. Difficult conversations or drama in our relationships can trigger our escapisms.

It may seem easier to stay busy rather than address something uncomfortable. I had the tendency in the past to make future moments too big as an excuse to avoid something I didn't want to face. For example, if I had an upcoming deadline or speech, I would tell myself something like "this isn't the right time to address an issue," therefore letting problems linger—which also let a lot of unnecessary stress run in the background. This creates procrastination through sweeping difficulties under the rug, hoping they'll go away.

They don't; they just become more difficult.

Anything that isn't addressed, due to fear of rejection, confrontation, or judgment, simply takes more time and in the long run destroys bandwidth, the ability to create. Escapisms destroy our capacity to create value and can cloud our vision, undermining our confidence. This will limit focus and reduce the ability to create maximum value; ultimately it limits power, and we are stuck back in a Shadow Persona.

Instead, address issues as they come up, and create the space for production and the environment for expression. (If you aren't clear about your escapisms, look to your complaints, the people you judge the most. See if there is a reason you have so much angst, anger, and if it might be a deflection from something you don't love about yourself.)

To eliminate escapisms from your life, simply do an assessment. Ask yourself, "What's not working, and how do I want it to work?" Do this regarding your health, relationships, finances, or any area. Ask yourself, "Is there any limitation?"

If I'm frustrated with someone and remain that way, it usually triggers an escapism: it's something to address, but maybe fear prevents me from doing it. Or maybe the issue exists because of something I have yet to see in myself. The fact that I am triggered is evidence that it is something that reminds me of some judgment I hold for myself. For example, if I'm pissed because someone lacks integrity, it could be that I have also been short on integrity. Holding onto scarcity thinking will create a wedge in the relationship and undermine your ability to think clearly and shift to a Winning Persona.

Here is how escapism works with me. My wife would want to talk about something important or difficult, but I would become too tired. As soon as she would start talking, I'd fall asleep. I'd fall asleep at eight thirty p.m. At first, I was convinced this was just because I had been busy and needed the rest.

Then one time, my wife and I were having a tough conversation, and the thought came to me, *Oh my God, I'm starting to get tired.* I said, "Babe, I'm going to sit up. We're going to turn on the lights." I wanted to check out and escape, but for the first time I realized I was in escapism, even though I'd previously believed my sleepiness was merely a physical response.

Here's another example: I sometimes wake up at three a.m., because from three to five a.m., nobody will bother me. I can watch something on TV and zone out. Other forms of escapism could be anything from watching porn to lying awake, worrying about everyone else's problems and taking them on so you don't have to face your own.

These forms of escapism are subtle, so we all tend to say, "I won't hold you accountable if you don't hold me accountable." I get to say I don't have the money, I don't have the time, or I've been really busy. I get to tell you about all my problems so that we don't have to deal with responsibility. That's an escapism.

We can find the time that we say we don't have by eliminating escapisms. This doesn't mean we're enlightened so we float around and these temptations never come up, but we become aware of them sooner and can correct course.

Bankruptcy is a forced correction. Divorce is a forced correction. Course corrections are taking responsibility, apologizing, learning, and then moving forward. Most people never learn because they sweep the problem under the rug, but the lesson gets harder, bigger, and more profound till we finally pay attention. I'd rather pay attention when it's a nudge rather than when it's a brick to the face. When ignored, these issues lead to discomfort, even depression.

Our escapisms require a great deal of energy. These are programs of stress running in the background, tugging at our emotions and energy at the expense of our abundance. This is why people walk around tired all the time, with chronic illness, depression, and disconnection, buying more things to feel better, and getting the next temporary hit of dopamine.

Before I understood this, I remember having a bad day and eating a pint of ice cream. I felt worse afterward, but for the second that the sugar hit my lips, it tasted so good. Of course, I was actually just eating my emotions. Other people drink or smoke marijuana every night.

Are these things okay recreationally? Probably, but not when they become a means of escape. Once again, no truth exists without a context. Is this habit an enhancement or a deterrent? Does it help us to enjoy a moment and celebrate, or does it numb us out?

One of our escapisms is workaholism. We can justify it—"this is really important" or "it's just for this project"—but it becomes habitual.

Eliminate escapism and take responsibility, otherwise it will undermine your ability to create value and your vision.

Step Three: Delegate

The third step to flip to a winning game is to *delegate*. Delegation is "hard easy" versus "easy hard." Easy hard is, "It's easier just to do it myself right now rather than having to explain it. It's easier to do it myself rather than hire someone. I don't have the time." That's easy now but hard later, when we've hit our bandwidth and we're exhausted.

Delegating is hard now, but easy later. If I want to delegate, I have to find someone who is both responsible and really good at what they do. That person also has to be someone that I enjoy working with.

> Tasks are like boomerangs. They just keep coming back around: Instead, delegate *roles*.

Most people think they're good at delegating, but they delegate tasks. Tasks are like boomerangs. They just keep coming back around: What do I do next, over and over? That becomes exhausting. Instead, delegate *roles*. When I have people on my team who will own a role, it removes the worry and frees me up to do what I do best.

By addressing escapism, you can recover and find more time. With this additional time, you can train and hire people to delegate to. This increased time and production allows for you to do what you do best, but to do this, hire people in their Winning Persona.

Often when people don't eliminate or delegate, they just take on more and more. They start slowing down, they have less brain capacity, they're frustrated, and they have resentment and bitterness: other people are succeeding, and they're not. They don't know when they're going to have time for anything else. They no longer enjoy their work; they just dream of retirement, winning the lottery, or selling their business.

Delegation is not offloading everything; it's saying, "What is it that I, and only I, could do? What can I do that I'm best at? What might I enjoy? What will give me some energy?" Vision can't be delegated. The team can contribute to it, but to delegate the vision would be a travesty.

I founded a financial coaching business called the Wealth Factory. Over time I realized I wasn't the best coach, that it didn't leverage my Money Persona or skills properly. As a creator, I love inventing something new instead of following a process for clients. Once I had this epiphany, I allowed the Mindful Managers and Planners to take over the coaching, and our business grew (as did my enjoyment of it).

Delegating creates space for your vision and for doing things that move the needle for you and those you serve. It creates enjoyment in the process and journey. This is the key to your quality of life, allowing you to utilize your money to protect and grow your energy by doing what you really want to do. You are doing things that engage you at a level where you feel satisfaction now, not just working for the outcome alone.

Step Four: Collaborate

The fourth step to a winning game is *collaborate*. It's about bringing in capabilities that the team didn't previously have. It goes beyond delegation and using a team to accomplish more together. Delegation can bring you support to perform better and be more efficient, but this is about bringing in capabilities that expand your vision. It is about acquiring skill sets to have more impact, excellence, or reach.

Team sports like football are collaborative efforts: the quarterback has a completely different ability from the left tackle, the center, the running back, and the wide receiver. You've also got coaches, general managers, owners, vendors, caretakers, and the networks that are broadcasting the game. Collaboration is bringing together everyone and everything required for the game to come to full fruition. Again, delegation is offloading things from your plate, whereas collaboration is bringing in capabilities that were never on your plate in the first place.

Find those people who are the Winning Personas that you are not. Find the ones missing from your team to accomplish more by utilizing their skills and leveraging yours. Is there something you hate doing or don't know how to do? I promise you there is someone else out there who loves it. Someone like the superintendent in charge of the sewage department, a literal crappy job, that couldn't stop passionately telling me about his work.

Co-creation is about getting started and gaining momentum, whereas collaboration is about a more comprehensive team and the strategic partnerships that are required to bring your vision to fruition. It is also about finding capabilities that you do not have yourself. Delegation initiates the process, but collaboration is required for full implementation with all phases of creation. Co-creation is your start; collaboration is the big finish.

Healing from the Pain of a Losing Shadow Persona

As you begin to shift from a Shadow Persona to a Winning Persona, you may start to get down on yourself about the choices you made in the past. You may be haunted by past mistakes, or mentally kick yourself for not getting this sooner. This can be a painful process.

Listen, very few people get this, and often it's not until they've had a tragic wake-up call, like I did, because most of the Western world caters to Shadow Personas. We're all in on it, spinning plates, running on hamster wheels, hoarding money, and ignoring our Soul Purpose. So how could you have figured this out earlier?

Don't be so hard on yourself. You're here, now. You're beginning. You're finding your way to freedom.

You don't need the tragic wake-up call. This *book* can be your wake-up call.

We can be held captive by the pain of the past, ruminating on the negative, those defining marks or stains that hold us back, that place where we store guilt and shame. A lot of sabotage comes from the pain of past experiences. I experienced this firsthand from my time as a High Roller.

When we do things for the wrong reasons, they don't work out; but let this be a teacher through experience. However long or hard the lesson is will be up to us. What are we trying to prove, or who are we trying to impress and why?

In the Consumer Condition, people would rather not make

a mistake but end up stuck in a losing game of avoidance or striving for perfection. In this game, people are not unique, we are not different. Without overcoming challenges or pain, what is there to learn and celebrate? Sure, we can learn without mistakes and pain, but often they are companions in the process.

Use your past to discover what matters most to you, to uncover your values, rather than be defined by your mistakes. The only way is to *know* your value and to *live* those values. Your values, when clearly defined and understood, are like a script into living a great life, taking a stand for what matters to you.

As you heal from your Shadow Persona, you may also feel guilt or shame about your past choices and how your behavior has impacted your relationships. And your relationships will start to shift. Those who are stuck in the Consumer Condition may not understand your new perspective. That's okay. They don't have to agree with you for you to accept and love them. You'll find others, new relationships that provide the support you need, and opportunities for collaboration. And you'll discover that, when you choose to connect to the people you love, rather than disconnect from them in pursuit of a losing game, your relationships get stronger.

Here is a seven-step process to heal pain and connect in relationships:

BE RADICALLY VULNERABLE: Virgil Knyght showed me this. He said, "I would have never guessed what a superpower being vulnerable was in my younger years." He let me know I was only responsible for my side of the equation. The key is to be open, share who you are with the world, and many will choose to do the same with you.

TAKE OWNERSHIP AND APOLOGIZE: A sincere apology connects with the authentic self. Where can you take responsibility for any pain you have caused or for actions that were less than ideal? Make a list of the people you would like to create a new story with, the people with whom you wish you would have handled something differently. Take the opportunity to acknowledge where you may have been immature, emotional, or simply harmful, and then reach out. This can be done through a letter or in person.

LISTEN: Want to know how to connect with people? Ask them about their story, discover their pain, and love on them. Care about them. Love and compassion are the key companions to heal from a Shadow Persona or damaged relationship. This step is about being quiet. This isn't about you. It isn't about solving anything or what you say; it's how you listen. Allow people to share their story, their scars, and their pain.

STAY PRESENT: As in step two of the flip, identify escapism and busyness. Overcome any excuses that prevent conversation. Excuses create stories that destroy connection. Be aware and stay present, as escapism may bring patterns or mechanisms from the past to avoid the pain. Be with the pain. Feel it and be willing to stay in it until you have experienced the full emotion. Don't try to escape until you reach the beauty of connection, the other side of the pain. Also, be careful not to suffer the future by worrying about the outcome or carrying something before it happens. It can limit the result. We are not responsible for the outcome; we are only responsible for having the courage to handle our side of the equation.

ASSESS THE PAIN: When the intensity of being uncomfortable increases or the fear is intense, especially if you feel defensive, ask yourself where the pain is coming from. How do you feel it and where? Where does it reside in the body? This can bring you into the present and become the gateway to healing.

FEEL THE CONNECTION: On the other side of the pain, we can find peace, energy, and be connected. Stand with strength, presence, and love until you find that spot within yourself or together in relationship. If the person you talk to doesn't want to participate or change, love them anyway. Sometimes that love may be from a distance—and that's okay.

CREATE A NEW CONTEXT: Now is the time to rewrite your story. This doesn't mean revisionist history where you pretend the past didn't exist or happen. This is a tool to heal the past and create a new future. What did you learn? How have you grown? How do you want this relationship to be moving forward? There is room for new contracts and new possibilities if both parties are brave enough to choose love and connect.

If the other party still feels emotional, angry, or unwilling to forgive, then go back to step one. You can choose how many times to do this. It may even be just once. Some people are ready to heal wounds, and some aren't. The key is in loving and forgiving yourself and avoiding the trap of sacrifice, or lingering feelings of unworthiness, guilt, or shame.

Give Yourself a Do-Over

The Seven-Step Process to Heal Pain and Connect in Relationships isn't required for each painful experience or moment. And it's not the only way you can heal relationships, or yourself. My friend Dino Watt introduced my wife and me to a powerful tool you may find useful, the Do-Over.

The Do-Over is one of the most instrumental tools Carrie and I have implemented in our marriage. When one of us says something dumb, gets hangry, and is temporarily insane or mean, when we *really* mess up, we can ask for a do-over, which acknowledges that we would behave differently if given the chance to *do it over again.*

In those moments where your emotions take over and you do something you immediately regret, use a do-over. It is also helpful in any relationship where past experiences keep finding a way into current arguments. A do-over is an opportunity to go back and acknowledge you got off on the wrong foot and to add love rather than pain. It's admitting that what you did was hurtful or selfish. Or just stupid.

Accepting the request for a do-over is an act of lasting forgiveness. It is like a mulligan in golf, when used properly, but never to be abused.

A do-over can also work for your relationship with yourself. When you think about past choices, mistakes, and other things you wish you wouldn't have said or done, can you let go of guilt and shame and give yourself a fresh start?

What do you want to do over? Where do you *need* a do-over?

The ROI on Joy and Love

Jessica Fay started a chiropractic practice at a time in her life when she hit rock bottom. Her engagement had ended, which meant she suddenly didn't have a place to live, and a job she had lined up in Atlanta to get her away from it all fell through days before she was about to move there. She picked up the pieces where she lived in Raleigh and tried to make a practice work there on her own.

Jessica threw herself into work more than ever before. "It became all-consuming," she told me. "I sacrificed everything else in my life to devote time to my business."

Over the years she'd grown from a solo practitioner to a successful practice with an associate chiropractor and five massage therapists. Despite her professional accomplishments, in 2019 she began to feel empty and didn't know why.

"Every day when I went to the office, it felt like I was sprinting a marathon, trying desperately to beat the previous week's numbers," Jessica said. "My self-worth had become very tied to whether or not the practice grew each week."

When COVID-19 hit, Jessica went from her busiest week ever in practice to the bottom falling out the following week. "I panicked for the first month or so, not knowing if I was going to be able to keep my team employed, or when or if patients would start coming back," she said. "But then I suddenly opened up to what I'd been resisting for a long time: creating space for a life and an identity outside of work."

By reconnecting to the experiences, people, and interests that brought her joy, Jessica began to heal from her losing Shadow Persona, the Striver. When you're struggling financially, or hitting brick walls in your business, it may seem counterintuitive to spend *less* time working on those issues. That resistance is rooted in scarcity thinking. We believe we can't solve financial problems by focusing on the things we love to do.

I wouldn't have believed it back in my Striver days. I would have doubled my efforts—and did just that many times—to get out of whatever hole I thought I was in. Sometimes the financial hell is real. We have bills to pay and creditors knocking on our doors. I've been there.

But often, the hole is one we have created for ourselves based on a false definition of success. And just so we're clear where that comes from, allow me to repeat myself—again: until we heal from our Shadow Personas, our definition of success is rooted in scarcity thinking. And so, it's not our definition at all, is it?

"I started riding my bike again on backcountry roads, I got a gravel bike to hit trails with, I started playing guitar and writing again," Jessica said. "My conversations with friends and family became less rushed and more meaningful. I spent more time on self-work and self-care. I finally started putting pictures on my walls and making my house a home. Even after I built the business back up after the virus, I kept my reduced office hours to protect more time for my life and identity outside of work."

By focusing on what and who she loved, by investing in her own joy and in her relationships, Jessica not only healed from the pain of her Shadow Persona; she also reached levels of growth in her business that she had not been able to obtain when she was in Striver mode.

"The wild part was," she said, "by stepping back and letting go, I had the most profitable year yet, even in a pandemic—almost double what I made by this time the previous year."

Jessica redefined her "win," and the success followed. In the next chapter, I'll show you how to define your own win *before* you play the game.

Unlock Hidden Capital

"He was so poor that all he had
left was his money."

—BOB MARLEY

L et's go back to the question: "What would you do with a billion dollars?"

A billion dollars.

That is far too much money to spend alone, but not enough money to sustainably change much in a world with almost eight billion people.

Money isn't powerful enough to solve the world's problems. To really solve the complex issues requires different forms of capital that money merely represents. Most of this capital goes unrealized and undetected, due to misinformation, myths, and limiting beliefs that keep it locked away and ultimately lost.

There are two more precious forms of capital that drive all financial capital. Without them, money would have no value whatsoever. It would be rendered useless. Money is merely a man-made tool of efficiency to tap into and access the real value. Knowing where this Hidden Capital is, how to develop it, expand it, and utilize it is the key to wealth. The key to creating your winning game.

The key to finally understanding and abolishing scarcity.

Are you ready?

First: Mental Capital

You are your greatest asset—not a bond, stock, or even a piece of real estate. Your Mental Capital is the key to unlock your asset, your value. Mental Capital includes:

> ❯ Education
>
> ❯ Experiences
>
> ❯ Insights
>
> ❯ Interests
>
> ❯ Tools
>
> ❯ Skills

mental capital:

The combination of your ideas and skills, your experience, emotional intelligence, and integrity. It's everything that you know.

Mental Capital is what you know. It's your ideas and the information you have. It's your emotional intelligence, your ability to connect with others and understand them. It's the skills that allow you to make your life better while bringing value to others, to make their lives better, or to offer them meaningful experiences. It can also involve creating a safe space where others can open up to you, or for you to be honest and vulnerable yourself.

Mental Capital accelerates with integrity. By being true to who you are, you unlock more of what you know. Instead of trying to mimic someone else, follow your path instead. Discover what drives you, and accelerate results by knowing what you love and what you do best.

Find your way.

Then, take that Mental Capital and become curious. What problems are you uniquely gifted to solve? In what ways are you compelled to naturally serve? Ask questions, stay in inquiry to find out what makes other people tick, discover what they care about.

But start with yourself.

Don't rush ahead. By knowing yourself you will be able to add the most value to others' lives.

When people skip the step of discovering themselves, what they love, where their interests are, and the abilities they can develop consistent with their desires, they lose.

Often this simply happens in the name of making money. To make a living, as they say, people limit their Mental Capital and ultimately diminish their life. Ironically and sadly, this causes them to lose long-term wealth and immediate fulfillment.

There are plenty of reasons this happens: financial surprises, family issues, health challenges, and myriad other difficult circumstances.

All of this can lead to trading time for money, hustling and grinding, or scrimping and sacrificing.

It's heavy.

It can be hard.

And in those moments, dreaming can feel impossible, even irresponsible, or just too far off, when every day is about survival.

Debt can drown out the best of who we are and blind us to the value we can create. Demonstrative statements from loved ones or divorce can drive our focus to detriment rather than development. There are plenty of reasons wealth isn't cultivated or Mental Capital isn't realized or found. The hidden cost is what is really lost.

Time.
Energy.
Memories.
Ability.

We lose life in the name of making money. Money without Mental Capital is shallow. Money before purpose skips the instrumental step, is temporary at best, and will never be sustainable.

Money without Mental Capital, money without value, is something for nothing. Luck, at best. It removes the joy from our life and destroys our winning game. The win is in the process, in the work; so why would we want to miss out on those moments for money?

To have a billion dollars without the Mental Capital would be short-lived. Look at the statistics on lottery winners. Many of them end up bankrupt, in jail, or worse. Money without Mental Capital is reckless and wrought with wrongdoing. It can blind us to purpose and remove the process of discovering who we really are.

What do you want to learn? Where do you want to develop and grow?

Money can be an asset or a liability, a deterrent or accelerant. If we earn it, it is a by-product of value. That value is mined from our Mental Capital. If money comes from the lottery, theft, or an inheritance—well, good luck. It can be a blessing or a curse. It really depends on the person, on the game they are playing, the value they are creating, and the life they are living. Money without Mental Capital is like a license without a car, a plane without a pilot, or a brush without an artist.

Developing your Mental Capital means discovering yourself

and the knowledge that you can uniquely share with others. Search for the things that you have an aptitude for and that you enjoy learning. Don't be misled. Don't try to shortcut your way to wealth.

The Consumer Condition is fueled by the notion that material wealth is the top priority, that sacrifice is the only way to succeed, and that you don't have time to invest, so just hand over your money (and therefore your life) to so-called experts. This diminishes your lifestyle and ignores your Hidden Capital. This untapped capital is within you, waiting to be harnessed to create a life you love.

Again, your most important asset is *you*—your character, passion, experience, knowledge, skills, ideas, insights. It's your ability to express value by tapping into the best of who you are. When you focus on your quality of life through learning and creating, that will allow you to create value for others. Wealth is the by-product of how you live and your perspective, and the product of a life well lived is value.

Invest in yourself, your life, and your experiences along the way. The more you value yourself, the more you honor yourself, and the more life starts to feel like play; you will naturally create more value for others.

> By living true to your values, to building a life you value, you will generate more wealth.

To account for, unlock, and identify your Mental Capital, start a list of your knowledge gained through education. This goes beyond a formal education, by the way. You may have taken informal classes, or learned from a mentor, or educated yourself by reading and listening. You also gain knowledge and perspective through experiences, so catalog those as well. These are not just experiences you chose to have, such as traveling abroad or interning. These could be experiences you *survived*. When you weather a storm, that's a valuable experience. Note the insights you've gained from these experiences.

Now consider the systems and tools you've developed or acquired. Jot them down. How have you adapted systems and tools for your own life and work? How do you use them differently? This is all *valuable*. Then, note the skills you have, both personal and professional. What do you know how to do? What do people ask you to do for them, because they don't know how to do it? Even if you think it's not something you could monetize, write it down.

In times where you lost money or a relationship, ask yourself: What would I have done differently knowing what I know now? What questions would I have asked if I could go back and do it again? This is key to capturing and sharing your Mental Capital. The toughest experiences can create the most meaningful value.

Next: Relationship Capital

Relationship Capital is the most valuable, yet underutilized, asset in the world. Relationship Capital comes from people—people who know how to create value and, most importantly, know how to receive and ask for value as well. It comes from those with whom you have built relationships (online and in person) and even the relationships from those you know, their network. Relationship Capital includes:

> Subscribers

> Customers

> Mentors

> Family

> Friends

> Team

relationship capital:

It comes from relationships (both online and in person) with people who create value and know how to ask and receive value.

What do people really value? Do you know? How can you deepen your relationship with others to find out? These conversations are so simple, yet we rarely have them.

Invest in people. In time. Energy. Value. Get to know them. Be present.

Do something fun, make them laugh, or show up in an unexpected way. Write a handwritten note or get with John Ruhlin and *Giftology* to send them an unforgettable customized, meaningful gift. Be generous with your compliments and let them know how they have impacted you. And, maybe easier said than done, allow them to support and impact you. When you support others, you feel more connected to them; now allow that for yourself.

In communication, you don't have to have an agenda or try and earn anything. Just open up. Just share.

Be real.

Be vulnerable.

Be perfectly imperfect.

Often people come across as arrogant when they want others to love them more than they love themselves. Stop trying so hard to impress people and just be yourself. Ask more questions. Have the confidence and abundance to listen and learn.

Sometimes this is hard to do; I definitely know. I recently met my favorite DJ, Steve Aoki, because of my friend Ross. For five minutes, well, I had diarrhea mouth.

I talked too fast.

I stopped listening.

I tried to impress and seem cooler than I am.

It happens. Ross and I laughed about it. I forgot to just be, allow for flow, and simply stay in the moment. I made it too much about me rather than Steve.

When we spew too much, it feels like an agenda or a one-way street—because it often is. I've been there. My wife has grabbed my knee under the dinner table so many times as a code to stop talking and just listen. The world of scarcity has us vying for attention and is so noisy we can forget how to stay in the moment, as we feel time is limited.

We often struggle to find the time for relationships when we try to do too much on our own. When we are trapped in scarcity and sacrifice, we rarely ask for help. "If you want something done right, you have to do it yourself." Isn't that the mantra of scarcity?

Think of all the time we take struggling and sacrificing to

save money by doing something ourselves. This limits our opportunity to tap into the abilities of others and develop Relationship Capital. We cheat ourselves and others by doing everything alone. Our herculean efforts can lead us to feel resentment and anger, often occupying our thoughts to the point we forget about other people. We crowd them out.

When we are exhausted, or in scarcity, we almost never have the ability to compliment someone else. Sacrifice is a path to exhaustion, resentment, and jealousy. It is a heavy burden. Humanity has been taught they shouldn't feel worthy of success; why? Because of the lie that is sacrifice.

Pay your dues, they say. They just got lucky, or knew someone, or don't deserve this, or blah blah blah. The weight and feeling of being financially behind or responsible for things outside of our control leaves remnants of shame. I should be further ahead. But on the other side of the coin, there is guilt for those who have "made" it.

Who am I to have this?

What else can I do?

Have I done enough?

There is that word again. Enough.

Enough is the fuel for sacrifice.

When we exhaust ourselves like the Miser trying to find **more** deals, or like the Conservative wanting to set aside **more**, or the Striver wanting to work **more**, or the High Roller wanting to have **more**, there isn't space for others. There isn't room for Relationship Capital.

A relationship can be built or destroyed in a moment. When we exhaust ourselves, we don't show up as the best version of who we are. Genuine acknowledgement of another is one of the fastest ways to bond and build a relationship, but scarcity rarely allows that to happen. To build Relationship Capital, it doesn't even have to be you who delivers the value. Ask yourself, "If I can't create value, who do I know who can?"

Take time to build relationships. Delegate as a way to free up your time and connect with those who are serving you. Unlock Relationship Capital by making a list of your constraints, distractions, and obstacles. Who do you know who can support you in solving these issues? Know this: If you have the money to solve the problem, then you don't have a problem. Unless scarcity won't let you part with your money, that is.

If you don't know who can help you, simply make a list of the people in your personal and professional network. Don't limit your list to people who are close to you; include acquaintances and other people you've had limited interactions with. Sometimes we think we "don't know enough people" or we don't know enough Catalysts. Everyone has value and Relationship Capital.

If there are people you want to know better, look at your list and figure out if anyone in your network is connected with them. Then ask for an introduction and develop the relationship. But start with your existing relationships.

Select some of the people to have a regular rhythm with: a phone call, a walk, or dinner on an ongoing basis. Carve out time, make space for them, and create rhythms. I've found blurring the lines between work and play is a key to Win, Then Play. We win when we play, but so often, we *don't* make time for the things we enjoy, for self-care, and the things that fill our tank. We say we "don't have time," and then everything becomes an effort.

So, I invite and integrate work into my daily life more often and make space for life in my work. I set up hikes with contacts who live in my area. I take my son with me when I film in Los Angeles. I set up immersive experiences at my favorite place—our cabin. I'm working and providing value, and I'm also doing things I want to do. I grill on my Traeger, walk the river, and feed the fish in my pond while enjoying great conversations.

Building Relationship Capital doesn't have to be a daunting or time-consuming endeavor, especially when you allow for support. When you delegate and collaborate, you can find time to invest in people. Share your favorite hobbies. Bring people you love and admire together.

The Value Equation: A Key to Win, Then Play

The Value Equation is the process of leveraging knowledge and engaging people to create profit.

$$\text{Mental Capital} \times \text{Relationship Capital} = \text{Financial Capital}$$

Another way of expressing it is knowledge plus people equals wealth. Therefore, **whenever we think we have a money problem, it isn't a money problem; it's a Mental or Relationship Capital issue**.

You might be one idea or one relationship away from the next level of prosperity, but make sure you are playing a game worth winning. Develop Mental Capital that matters to you and with relationships (Relationship Capital) you enjoy.

Some see borrowing as the best (or only) way to grow financial capital. However, borrowing money or raising capital takes time and can be an unnecessary step in the value creation model.

Win, Then Play makes it possible to build financial capital without borrowing, by adding value instead. Leveraging financial capital can be dangerous. People who leverage and borrow money without knowledge take unnecessary risk. They are susceptible to hype and greed and often learn expensive lessons. So, when it comes to financial capital, don't borrow it, except in times of emergency or to take advantage of the rarest opportunities.

A lot of business executives and start-ups are taught to raise financial capital. Few are taught to raise their Mental and Relationship Capital first.

I want to drive this home: people love the opportunity to serve and support things they value. What they can support, they will support.

Be a Value Creator

Roberto Monaco lives the Value Equation (MC $*$ RC $+$ FC). My friend Phil Tirone came to one of my speeches. At the end of the event, he asked me, "Would you like people to do something as a result of what you are teaching?"

Of course, I thought that would be fantastic. He introduced me to Roberto, and we scheduled a full-day strategy session around his concept of Influenceology.

Unfortunately, my partners died that month and I canceled. But his name came up again when one of my clients and a huge Catalyst in my life, Garrett J. White, met him at a mortgage event. Garrett and I chose to hire Roberto the day of Garrett J. White's Cash Flow Club. After Roberto's coaching, eighty-eight out of the 128 people in attendance bought tickets to a second event I was hosting a week and a half later.

Even better, Roberto filmed this event, went back to my office, and worked until three thirty a.m., breaking it down frame by frame. Roberto is so committed to value it feels like he overdelivers all the time, which makes him easy to refer.

I introduced him to Dr. Patrick Gentempo, a Catalyst in the chiropractic world. Roberto didn't even know what chiropractic meant. Through his encounter with Dr. Gentempo, Roberto is now the top provider on influence and speaking in the profession. He launched the Chiro Speaking Club, and now 70 percent of his business comes from chiropractors. Due to his training, 1,500 new people go through chiropractic treatment each month.

These are just two of the more than one hundred people I have introduced to Roberto by direct referral. He has gotten exposure to thousands more because I interview him, mention him from stage, and discuss him in situations like this book.

When you build Relationship Capital by supporting or promoting people of value, it can create even more Relationship Capital. It lends credibility and creates faster results for both parties involved. No compensation changes hands, but there's an immense feeling of gratitude between us.

The lesson: be referable. Add value in all situations for your Relationship Capital list. Know your value first, then be a value creator, and it will be easy for friends to connect you with their relationships, knowing their friends are in great hands.

Over time, you will find that the value you receive reflects the value you give and who you are.

Honor Your Word

The government can't tax your Relationship Capital. But something that can take years to develop can be destroyed in a moment if you don't do what you say you'll do. The key to building—and, most importantly, sustaining—relationships is integrity. If it isn't possible to keep your word in a given situation, honor it by staying in communication to create new expectations, possibilities, or to recruit support. Relationships are built and strengthened one commitment at a time, over long periods of time.

Sometimes when things don't go as planned, people get scared. Rather than being proactive, people are often reactive, which destroys Relationship Capital. Be willing to tell the truth, even when it is hard or not what you hoped would happen. If you aren't going to meet a deadline or something doesn't go as planned, get in communication as soon as possible. Through proactively reaching out, you can create a new plan and honor your word by building a new agreement. Sure, this may not be possible every time. But if they are upset when you let them know ahead of time, imagine how much worse it could go if you wait too long.

This is one of the harder things to do: communicate difficult news. I remember everything crashing around me in 2008. My business was down for the first time since I started ten years earlier. I struggled to make payroll, could barely cover the mortgages on my rentals, and wondered if I could keep everything afloat. I could see that paying people on time was going to be difficult. I lost sleep, gained weight, and my hair started going gray. I was irritable, frustrated, and detached.

Worrying wasn't going to solve anything, so I picked up the phone. Rather than trying to ignore issues while the stress ran in the background, I finally addressed them directly. Procrastinating tough conversations was creating more pain and taking more time anyway, so I made the tough choice to be honest and face my fear.

This is the path to preserve Relationship Capital, especially when facing adversity. Adversity can be one of the greatest teachers as well. It takes courage to be proactive and admit our shortcomings. By letting those people know that payments could be late and I was working to solve the issue, we made it through. I was able to transform the time spent on worry and instead focus on production and solutions.

Honor your relationships by honoring your word and having the difficult conversations.

Connect with Authenticity

Far too many people don't know how to benefit from their Relationship Capital. It goes against their nature to ask for, let alone accept, support. Their goodwill/RC never moves from potential to production. They miss out on opportunities because they're too afraid to open up to others and let them know what's going on. They put up a façade and pretend everything is okay.

But their honesty could actually open doors for them. To build Relationship Capital, we have to be willing to tell the truth, admit our mistakes, and be of value. No one expects perfection; if they do, they are free to invest in new relationships. Authenticity is the currency that facilitates connection.

Often when people support you, it can be of tremendous value to them and to your relationship. In 2022, I hurt my back to the point I was bedridden for thirty-six hours. Support was required. Any movement caused my back to seize. In this scenario I reached out to anyone and everyone who might be able to help, which provided miraculous results. Dr. Craig Buhler made a house call and was able to get me to my feet. Tawnya, a life coach to whom I had added value in the past, moved appointments and came to see me right away. After I shared so much gratitude for her, she said, "This is a gift for me, to be in your presence, to invest time together." Wow, I was asking for support, she was of immense value, and yet it opened up my perspective even further. The experience bonded us; it was valuable to her as well.

Start from Where You Are

When we don't develop our Mental Capital, we want everyone else to make our decisions for us. We lose touch with our lives, our voice, and our winning game. When we neglect to discover our Mental Capital, we envy what others have because of what we have yet to find in ourselves. Value is found in people. The value of all the people on this planet cannot be distilled into a dollar amount, because people are inherently valuable, and math and money cannot quantify what matters most—a moment. A kiss. An act of kindness. Art for the sake of expression. And most valuable and abundant of all, love.

You may have limited financial capital at the moment, but you have unlimited Hidden Capital *right now*. You can start with no money and become a millionaire and beyond, by leveraging your most fundamental and valuable asset: YOU.

This means that when it comes to building wealth, the most important investments come from knowing yourself. Invest in yourself—cultivate good habits, expand your knowledge, develop your skills, and focus on what brings you fulfillment.

CHAPTER

The Cycle of Creation

"Here's to the crazy ones. The misfits. The rebels. The troublemakers. The round pegs in the square holes. The ones who see things differently. They're not fond of rules. And they have no respect for the status quo. You can quote them, disagree with them, glorify, or vilify them. About the only thing you can't do is ignore them. Because they change things. They push the human race forward. And while some may see them as the crazy ones, we see genius."

—Made famous by STEVE JOBS

You've probably heard the common phrase "it takes money to make money" more than a thousand times in your life. And maybe you believed it, or still do. Maybe you have a business plan or a list of ideas or product launches that never got off the ground because you thought you didn't have enough seed money. Or maybe you didn't even let yourself get to the planning stage, because you believed you'd never raise the funds anyway.

Anyone who tells you that "it takes money to make money" wants your money, and anyone who believes this doesn't have a full understanding of what true assets are. It doesn't take money to make money—it takes ingenuity, resourcefulness, and value creation. By now, I hope you see that much of the financial and business "truths" are rooted in scarcity thinking and perpetuated by people living in their Shadow Personas. If you bought into the conventional wisdom that it takes money to make money, that's okay. You can make different choices going forward.

At some point, most of us have been advised to "live within our means," and generally, that's wise. The problem is that most people try to incorporate it into a Playing Not to Lose strategy—to live the advice, they cut back and budget. But the smartest way to live within your means isn't to think in terms of *re*duction, but in terms of *pro*duction. To use a common economic metaphor, instead of eating less pie, learn how to bake a bigger pie.

If you're struggling, it's easier and smarter to expand your means by increasing production and value creation for others. This means investing in yourself to get better at solving problems and serving others. Enhance your skills and advance your abilities. Use the Win, Then Play methodologies to prove your ideas profitably up front.

Those who Play Not to Lose rarely focus on problem solving or generating value to drive income. Distracted by fear, doubt, worry, or uncertainty, they obsess on how to use their current means, rather than expanding those means. However, human ingenuity illuminates new ways to use those resources. A piano has eighty-eight keys. But with those limited keys, you can create unlimited melodies. Like piano keys, it may seem to you like your resources are limited. But your ability to create value is unlimited.

To expand your means, ask yourself questions like:

> How can I deliver more value?

> What methods can I use to reach more people?

> How can I impact people more deeply?

> How can I solve the problems I see people struggling with?

When you expand your means with Win, Then Play, you do so by profiting up front without investing a single dime and in a minimal amount of time. This begins with the Cycle of Creation and then utilizes the technology of the presell so you never have to borrow money for your business or projects again.

This step-by-step process will help you take an idea to concept and build a framework that delivers a product, service, or experience in the marketplace regardless of your current financial situation. Using this methodology, people have written books, made documentaries, and created physical products without having to present to Silicon Valley investors or put up a single penny of their own.

Instead of investing your own money, you get paid up front by those who benefit from what you are building. No wasted time with investors, no forfeiting ownership, and no repaying capital through production. This gives you the cash flow to take ideas to market faster, create immediate momentum, and raise money through purchase rather than equity or debt.

You don't have to spend time raising funds, give away equity in your business, or take on unnecessary risks with your own cash to realize your Value Index vision. The antidote to the "takes money to make money" losing game is the Cycle of Creation. It is a duplicable process, so you gain confidence as you advance one win at a time and steadily grow both your vision and your cash flow. You'll save time, make money on your ideas before investing a single cent, and create momentum rather than debt in your business.

Utilizing the Cycle of Creation unveils potential obstacles before they occur and discerns opportunity from distraction. It is a conscious, deliberate way to take on a new project, create a new product, or grow your business.

The Cycle of Creation engages your Mental and Relationship Capital, to collaborate with others and focus on what you do best. You identify the best opportunities, then build them into immediate revenue streams or abandon them before spending substantial time or money. The process breaks down into four steps:

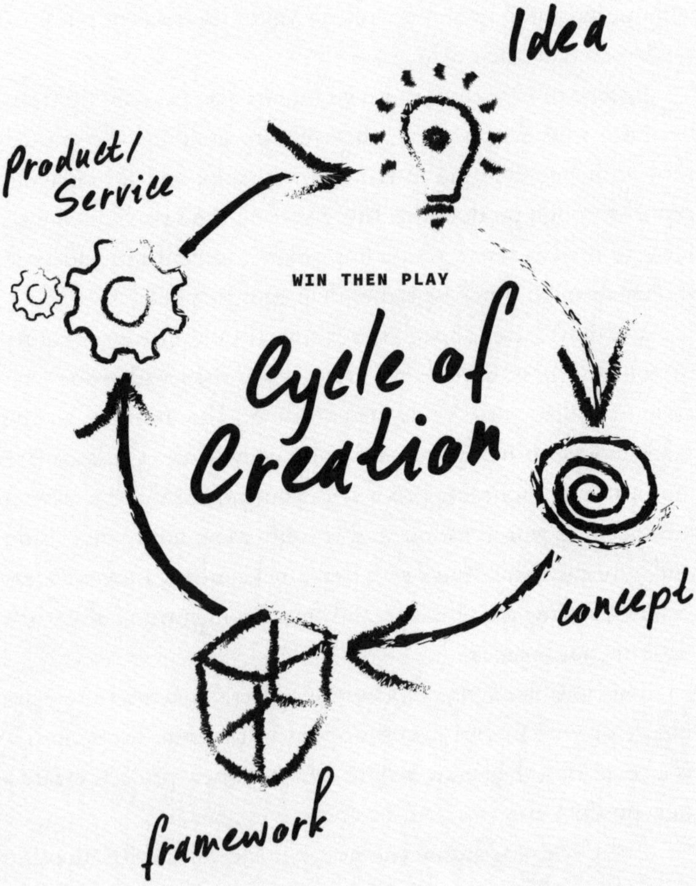

Idea

Product/
Service

WIN THEN PLAY

Cycle of
Creation

concept

framework

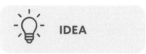

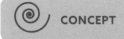

The Cycle of Creation is my favorite methodology for momentum, profit, and risk reduction. I used it to sell 22,000 copies of my first book, *Killing Sacred Cows*, before it was finished. I used it to create $150,000 of revenue for my first video program before we filmed it. And I created a course to implement the concepts in this book by doing a few interviews with Catalysts and preselling the recordings to their databases. To show you how doable this is, Ian Stanley interviewed me for an hour, and from that recording alone we had $17,000 of presells from his database.

Let's go over each step so you can start the process right away.

Step One: Brainstorm and Analyze Ideas

Start with vision. This phase is not about asking "how" or "when"; instead ask, "what will this idea do?" and "why this idea?"

Question the status quo. What do you see that others don't? In what ways do you have the excitement and energy to invent or improve? Tap into your Mental Capital.

If you aren't sure what to invent, ask, "What problems do people face?" If money, time, or ability weren't a limitation, what problems would you want to solve? Once you've identified people's pain and problems, you can brainstorm solutions and ideas. This requires both empathy and vision. You're not looking for the final or perfect idea at first; every original idea will evolve over time as you get feedback. What matters isn't your ability to come up with perfect ideas, but rather your ability to turn bold ideas into genuine value propositions that really work. Get as many ideas out as possible, then analyze them to identify the best ones. You may discover or download ideas while enjoying your hobbies, having a conversation with a friend, or even when you are dealing with something inefficient that you want to improve.

 Once you have an idea you want to run with, check in with yourself. If money were of no concern, would you still do this idea? Is this idea in alignment with your Soul Purpose and your Value Index? Will it help you realize your vision and live a life you love? Or is the idea solely about making money, gaining recognition, or beating your competition? If it's the latter, remember, you can only win a game worth playing, and sometimes your win is to never begin.

Take the time to find what is aligned, what calls forth the best of who you are.

Step Two: Turn Ideas into Concepts

A concept bridges the gap between an idea and a plan. It refines your sense of how you're going to add value in a way you can easily explain. An idea becomes a concept when it is shared with others, focusing to be more detailed and specific. You know you have a solid concept when you can clearly and succinctly describe the essence of the business to others in two or three sentences. My friend Rich Christiansen says his rule of thumb is this: If you can't describe your concept in a way that a ten-year-old can understand quickly, then you haven't developed it enough.

This book began as I was mentoring a friend and client. She was looking for options to create more freedom, embrace innovation, and express her inner artist. I shared my personal philosophy of Win, Then Play. She loved it and didn't understand why I hadn't written about it before.

I had launched video courses with Wealth Factory like Financial Trends Summit, Freedom FastTrack On-Demand, and even programs like Wealth Builders Club, all using Win, Then Play. But I hadn't shared the process with the public. I did have one workbook that we shared with a few of our clients years before, but everything expanded when I started talking about it on podcasts, webinars, and in my speeches. At that point, the idea became more concrete, and once I wrote the outline, it evolved into a concept.

Many business owners find it easier to come up with ideas than to implement them. The concept stage allows you to test which ideas have legs. For example, I once tested a business productivity course with one of my early mentors, Rick Sapio. Rather than filming everything, building the workbooks, and then trying to sell the course, we had a meeting, wrote an outline, and filmed three of the twenty-plus videos. We planned to test our concept from the stage at an event with nine hundred people.

We ran out of time to make the offer during our presentation. Through this, we realized the collaboration involved too much complexity and we didn't function efficiently together. We didn't create the course together. This saved time, money, and frustration. Rick went on to create the course Business Finishing School, with another friend, Patrick Gentempo. I even ended up contributing in my preferred way, by speaking at their events. It worked out with less effort, money, time, or struggle by testing it before fully building it.

To develop your ideas into concepts, start by thinking about the benefits of your product or service, who will buy it, how it will be sold, how it's different/better than others, and how you'll deliver it. Fleshing that out allows you to evaluate it more clearly for potential challenges and pitfalls. I typically write an outline at this phase, whether it's a book idea, a one-on-one program, a video series, or a marketing initiative—anything that is going to be offered in exchange for money.

Here are a few basic questions to help you develop ideas into clearer, more concrete concepts:

> What is my product/service and who will buy it?
> Why will they buy the product/service? How does it benefit them?
> How will the product/service be promoted and sold/offered?

As you answer these questions, you may find that your concept evolves. Or you may even eliminate it altogether.

Use some Relationship Capital to co-create and enhance this process. This may be as simple as running your concept past trusted mentors and advisors, or perhaps even potential customers (often the best feedback comes from those writing checks).

When writing this book, I created a reader group that not only gave feedback, but it also created a group of advocates who became case studies and even began promoting the book. One of my favorite ways to Win, Then Play is to create momentum during the concept phase. An amazing way to create profit is when your customers are enticed to buy before a product or service is available to the marketplace. One technique is preselling. Cathryn's Best Self Co. sells posters and shirts with a pop culture theme. As she was sharing a design idea for a journal with someone, they suggested using Kickstarter to launch the product. Knowing that small orders typically carry a higher cost than larger ones, she saw the potential to get the price break from the larger order. She launched her campaign before putting any money into the product, hoping to raise enough cash from future buyers to order one thousand units. Essentially, her buyers became her investors by purchasing the product before she made it. She sold one thousand units within twenty-eight hours. When all was said and done, Cathryn had raised enough money to reinvest the crowdsourced profits and produce thirty thousand units, which reduced the production costs by two thirds.

Kickstarter is just one way to presell your product, service, or experience. Andrew Drish has mastered the Win, Then Play strategy called Preselling. He breaks the process into five categories:

THE PITCH: Figure out how much money is required to launch the first version of your idea.

THE BENEFITS: Offer benefits that only founding members will ever get. Examples:

> Access to you

> Additional features

> Lifetime access to the product

> Discounts on all future products

THE CATCH: What you want in return for the reduced price or increased benefits. Examples:

> Give us a testimonial

> Let us use you as a case study

> Refer three friends if you love the product

The key is to make the benefits long and awesome & the catch short and easy.

THE TRACK RECORD: Give evidence of things in the past you created so they can trust you more. Examples:

> Past business success

> Features in press, media, podcasts, etc.

> Testimonials from other influential people who can vouch for you

> Proof you've built something like this before

THE GUARANTEE: give them a refund if they don't get what was expected to reassure them of making the investment. Examples:

> If you don't love it when it arrives, we'll refund your money

> Sign up today, try it for a month, and pay after you've used it

Using the Win, Then Play methodology, you start taking money as you refine your concept. You involve your customers in the process. You engage them, survey them, and get feedback along the way. With your concept clearly defined, you have an opportunity to delegate. The best way to delegate isn't by task, but with a framework.

Step Three: Build a Framework

A framework provides a blueprint for implementing your refined concept. The Creator's vision initiates the process, and the framework makes the vision a reality without requiring you to be involved moment by moment or step by step. It involves identifying the systems and peo-  ple with leverage. Without a framework, people often get trapped in hustle, working hard, and Playing to Win. A framework details how other people will be involved and gives them the tools to build this for and with you.

At this point, the Winning Persona of the Planner's gifts are best utilized by taking over for the Creator through handling the how and when with operations and administration. The Planner is a systems-oriented manager. They create policies and procedures that make operations run smoothly.

Planners can resist change because it threatens perfectly ordered systems. Thus, the Planner often feels frustrated by the Creator. But, without the Creator's vision, there would be minimal change or progress. And without the Planner, there would be no organization or implementation.

If you don't have the cash to build the framework, use the

presell, then reinvest some of the profits in hiring independent contractors part time to support you until it makes sense to hire someone full time. Some people give up equity and bring in a partner to do this. This can work but is dangerous, as it usually ends up in a Play to Win scenario where one person is doing more work than the other or is more committed than the other. If you go the partner or equity route, consider starting on a trial basis, and have exit strategies to protect you in the event this doesn't work as planned.

The Architecture of Production

The framework breaks the concept up into the tasks and processes required to implement the concept. With those identified, the Creator knows how to delegate each part to the Planner and the team, so that the implementation isn't just up to you. Remember, if you move from concept directly to building this on your own, complexity, chaos, and busyness will inevitably ensue.

If your Winning Persona is the Mindful Manager or Planner, look to team up with Creators and Catalysts to create more wealth through collaboration.

In the framework stage, you have the chance to ask questions before you are in the thick of things. This will not only allow you to cut through all this noise but will also allow others to support your vision. The framework begins by asking questions like:

> ❯ What is the simplest version of the product or service that can add value to people's lives?

> ❯ Who do you know that has the ability to do the things you don't want to do, or you don't have time for?

> ❯ Do you know of an organization that can benefit from this product/service/experience that may be able to support the creation?

Step Four: Take a Product, Service, or Experience to the Marketplace

With your framework created, now it's time to take your idea to market as an actual product, service, or experience. At this point, you're certain you can monetize your idea, because you already have customers. If you don't already have a database of subscribers or fans, you can start by offering your product or service to Catalysts—those influential relationships with those who can become spokespeople for what you do and your greatest referrers.

You implement the framework you've created and refine it over time to improve reach, productivity, and leverage. Use the funds from earlier stages to pay for those supporting the framework.

Cathryn used crowdfunding for version 1.0 of the journals she created. Then, she looked toward a longer-term vision, took the profits, and engaged and surveyed the initial buyers.[1]

---

1   This becomes a more sustainable business model than crowdfunding alone because you keep delivering more value to your existing customers.

The next cycle included the end user as part of the framework, which takes an idea and makes it multidimensional by adding value to the initial buyers. They opened a Facebook group, which created engagement. She asked what they valued. At first it was things that went along with the journal—accessories like a leather cover. Cathryn explained, "The journal is the tier A product, then we created tier B and C products to support the journal. Things like a 150-card prompt deck for the journal or an Edison deck of cards to support idea creation."

She created a graduate challenge to get people to use the product. If people used the journal for thirty days, there was a rebate system where they received a $10 Amazon gift card. This drove engagement and generated content from customers, who posted pictures that were then used for marketing. The community began to engage each other rather than the founders, initiating new ideas and building support for the product.

One issue with Best Self Co. journal came from people not knowing how to begin. Cathryn then took that feedback to create a product to support people getting started with the journal. "We found that most people don't talk about their daily routine normally, and this created new support and tapped into new Relationship Capital."

Remember: people love to help support that which they help to build. Customers developed habits around consuming Best Self Co. products. They came back for more and gave valuable feedback along the way.

The Cycle of Creation in Action

Here's how I launched my first video series, Freedom FastTrack On-Demand. At first, it was just an idea. Then, I created an outline for the course and knew what I wanted to teach. I did tele-seminars, recorded videos, and wrote articles, which helped me move from idea to concept. I gave talks on this topic and brain-stormed. I presold the video course before it was even finished.

Next, I moved into the framework stage, where I added Rela-tionship Capital to tap into Mental Capital I didn't have. I hadn't filmed a course before and wasn't used to doing video. I hired an editor and enlisted a co-creator, Garrett J. White. He had been a client, then came to work for me as my CEO and lead coach (and he is a world-class speaker). We did the videos together, co-created the workbooks, and he added content and insights to the outlines. Then I hired a sales team, who helped me map out a complete marketing campaign, sales script, survey, and process to reach out to those who were interested in the course.

I was confident the course would succeed when it launched because I had already proven the concept. It was a matter of utilizing Mental Capital and Relationship Capital along the way to get $150,000 of orders with the presell.

I identified the team required to produce the basics of the idea. This begins as the most basic version that provides value.

You may have several ideas of how to grow your business or launch a new idea. By using the Cycle of Creation, you uncover and take advantage of market demand first, instead of throw-ing ideas against the wall and hoping they will stick. You know exactly where to focus your efforts, recovering time to enhance your quality of life.

Reclaim Time

"It takes considerable knowledge to understand
the extent of your own ignorance."

—THOMAS SOWELL

T ime is money.

　　When you hear that, how does that make you feel? Like you should be doing something? That you might be behind on things? Time is ticking? That there is never enough time or money?

This phrase is said so often, by so many people, we've come to accept it as a fact.

But is it?

If you trade time for money—if you punch a clock or if you rely on "billable hours" to fund your business—then I suppose the belief that "time is money" has some merit. And yet, that phrase and ideology impacts nearly every aspect of life, not just work.

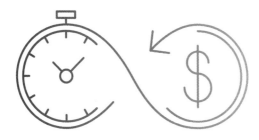

The time-is-money trap comes from linear thinking, the type of thinking that working harder must mean making more money. But what is work? The things we do for money? Does work only count when we are getting paid in the moment? If that were true, then what about vision, delegation, energy management, and even fun? Laboring without vision lends to the thought that time is money. And *time is money* leads to burnout.

Have you noticed how many articles and books there are on burnout? This is partly because when we follow the "time is money" mentality, there is no room for any activity that is not considered productive.

Time with friends.

Time to relax.

Time to play, and learn things, or be in nature.

Time to think.

To just *be.*

"Time is money" is something a Striver would say. That's why they are so busy and end up exhausted.

The other Shadow Personas have destructive ideas about time too. You might hear a Miser say, "I don't have time for that," because they hoard time like they hoard money. They need every moment of time to save money by researching and doing things themselves. The Conservative says, "There will be time for that later, in retirement." They often do work they hate and save enjoyment for an occasional vacation, and for that long stretch of nothingness they call "someday." The High Roller has short deadlines because that once-in-a-lifetime deal is always imminent, so hurry up or miss out. They are always promoting opportunities with time scarcity, and act quickly because these deals "won't last, must be done, and act right away." They say, "Time is slipping away."

The truth is, time is an artificial construct.

It was created to be a useful tool, and sometimes it is, in the right context.

We need to meet up—what time?

What time is your flight?

This project is due—what is the deadline?

And yet, that construct can become a problem. For example, when I scheduled the comedy tour, the one I shared in chapter 3, I set a date without thinking about how it would impact my life. My collaborators ran with it, and before I knew it, I was in overdrive trying to meet a meaningless deadline, sacrificing quality of life and stressing myself out.

Looming deadlines can leave minimal room for any other aspect of life. Avoiding deadlines ends up creating a stagnant feeling. Ideally, you will use time as a tool to coordinate, connect, and find your flow. In this chapter, I'll help you reclaim your time so you can use it to maximize your Mental Capital, Relationship Capital, and build a life you love, living your vision.

Time Is Not Linear

It can be tough to act on our Value Index vision with the obligations, noise, and busyness of the world. Often a vision comes without immediate payoff. In the trading time for money, salary, or hourly work model, there is an immediate payoff and immediate reward. Vision may take longer to realize. This is why people so often act before they are ready. When we put activity before intention, or work before thinking, it is easy to lose time, feel limited with time, or feel overwhelmed.

In the world of value creation, effort and time are not linear. Results are not directly related to the amount of time or how difficult the work is. For many this feels unfair. People cry for regulation, redistribution, and even socialism. For example, physical labor can be hard work, yet it is limited in leverage and pay. Someone may work longer hours, or do more excruciating work, and yet make less than someone who shares ideas and frameworks for the masses. My dad was a coal miner. That is much more dangerous and difficult work than what I do. So it may seem unfair that I make so much more than a coal miner. But value determines the payout; time determines the wage. Get beyond time for money and labor for dollars.

Money can be misleading when it tempts us to chase it—at the expense of our time, at the expense of our vision, and ultimately at the expense of our life. When we are trapped in the busyness of the world, it is difficult to hear the inner voice that guides us, much less take the time to listen to it. Listening, for me, is the hardest thing to do. How much time do you spend alone with your thoughts?

Instead of doing, I release trying to accomplish something, or impress someone, and just sit quietly. I focus on my breath. I meditate. I take a walk. I swim. I tinker around the garage.

Start by saying to yourself, there is nothing to do, nowhere to be; just be.

Take time to listen. Find that inner voice. Progress over perfection.

I remember my first meditation lasted less than sixty seconds. The other voice, the loud voice, my ego, urgently convinced me something needed to be done immediately, and I caved to the distraction. It may take practice, but it definitely takes intention and commitment. It is a different kind of muscle. It isn't about lifting or accomplishing or doing; it is about receiving. Allowing. Surrendering.

Find your process; discover what works best for you. You may be excited to act on all you've learned in this book so far, ready to step into your Winning Persona, leverage your Mental and Relationship Capital, and begin the Cycle of Creation, but first, listen.

Make and invest time.

Create space.

Make it possible for you to notice the gentle nudge, the gut feeling, or light feather to the face that is guiding you. The quiet voice.

Beyond Time Management

If we don't make the rules for how we use our time, society will make them for us and steal our flow. Reclaiming time is about finding your flow. Flow is exponential, not linear. Quality of life is personal; value is perspective, and living a life you don't want to retire from redefines timelines. Structure your life to have time and space for creativity, for thinking, for harmony, and for yourself. We become our habits, and when we sacrifice time for commitments and activities that don't provide value or meaning in our life, we end up *losing* our life.

When I do full-day immersions with clients, we start with a walk by the river, maybe a good latte and conversation, and then we get clear on our initiatives, our objectives. When people have more than five objectives, it's easy to get overwhelmed. A long to-do list takes up too much space in our minds and causes worry. Getting clear on objectives helps organize thoughts and gives them a place to live in time and space, which also creates natural ways to be more productive.

Separate your thoughts and action items into the following categories:

DOING. What are the things to do in the next two weeks? Rather than create a task list, add it in time and space in your calendar. Build a support team over time to get the project finished, then utilize co-creation, delegation, and collaboration to advance it.

LATER. Jot down the actions to take eventually. Use a journal, or an app on your phone, and move them to your calendar later. You may find that you end up delegating them to someone else or eliminating them entirely.

NEVER. What are the things you will no longer do? Maybe something is a great idea, but now that you know your Value Index, it no longer fits. Maybe it's something that doesn't move the needle for your Soul Purpose. Give it up and get it out of your mind and off your calendar.

PARKING LOT. Here, put your "someday" ideas, the fruits of your brainstorms. Allot space for what might come up without any concern for how and when. Details can bog people down and stifle creativity. Take the pressure off having to produce quickly.

You can review your parking lot and later categories as frequently as you would like.

Say No to Opportunities That Drain You

Do you ever find yourself so busy you don't know where to start or where you are spending more time talking about all you have to do rather than doing it? The "No Principle" is predicated upon knowing your purpose and shedding the "need" to sacrifice. "No" only works when you know when to say "yes." The first step, therefore, is to have a clear vision of who you are, what you want to do, and the life you want to craft. Create a game worth winning, and stay completely focused on that game. Know your win. This creates a standard by which all opportunities are measured. With that standard, it is easier to discern opportunities from distraction.

We are swimming in opportunity. We have to learn to stop saying yes to good ideas that crowd out the opportunity for great ones. The more we say "yes" to opportunities that are good but not right for us, the more diffused our energy becomes, the less power we have to fulfill our Soul Purpose. You can't say "yes" to purpose unless you repeatedly say "no" to distractions. You can't fully leverage your passion when scattered. Opportunities that are potentially lucrative but are outside our purpose are addictive but unfulfilling.

> My advice? Learn to say no.

My advice? Learn to say no. Win, Then Play is about being on the right journey, your journey. When you know the game you are playing, the game worth winning, you have the clarity to remove distractions disguised as opportunities. Saying yes to societal success may mean saying no to fulfillment, health, family, and to life success—your ultimate win.

Be careful with "maybe" as well. A maybe requires space in the mind. Energy for another time. We are usually decided but afraid of the answer. Listen to the inner voice in that moment. Are you afraid to say no? Is it just to people please that you keep the door open? My rule had to become a yes or no, because a maybe is where I would tend to overcommit and undercommunicate, making it impossible to be present. A maybe would lead to chaos and frustration—eventually. So, go with yes or no, never a maybe. Use the parking lot for tasks or projects that are a no for now.

Be Conscious in Relationships

We have enough *time and energy* to get everything done that we want to—if we don't hoard our money. People often save money and spend time. They try to do everything themselves to reduce expenses, but this requires a withdrawal of energy. If we protect our time from people who are energy drains or who don't share our values, we have plenty of time. Recognizing that someone doesn't share our values isn't a judgment of their character. It's simply being conscious of how we invest our time and energy to maximize our fulfillment, vision, and quality of life. An easy test can be when someone calls or texts. Do you want to answer, or do you dread the conversation? Do they uplift or drain you? How do you feel after the call?

Sometimes as business grows, the people who started with you are no longer a cultural fit or they don't want to grow past the first iteration of your vision. This is where business gets hard.

We grow attached to people, even when the skill sets or values aren't a fit. As crazy as it sounds, some people may even want you to fail because your success reminds them of something they don't know how to confront or work toward.

It can be even more painful and complicated when it happens with a relative. I've been accused of changing. It impacted the relationship. Sometimes that can be from the judgment of the person working on themselves, and that is a trap. I've been there too.

We all have our own path and our own pace. So much time is wasted in judging others rather than developing ourselves. At times people choose not to change or grow, because of the fear they could lose a relationship. They could lose their community or identity. If they don't stay the same, it could impact their family. This can happen when someone leaves a religion or shares that they are different in some way. Being true to ourselves can have massive implications because if those people we care most about succumb to fear, rather than love, we feel held back. It can require an astounding amount of time and energy to suppress our true selves. Expecting loved ones to do something so that it reflects well on us, or is what we want from them, is a demonstrative form of censorship. Removing freedom and pushing judgment on others is crippling. Where is the connection in that?

We lose time.

We lose expression.

We lose relationships.

Remaining unexpressed is Playing Not to Lose. What is more difficult, not being yourself and staying small to avoid judgement, or risking upsetting someone else? There will always be judgment, and the harshest may be what you say and feel about yourself.

Let love in.

Choose to love yourself and be who you are. Some people may understand, and others may not. It can be difficult, but there is no freedom in pretense and people-pleasing.

I have shared things with people I care deeply about where I worried about the outcome. Would I lose everything? Well, if I didn't speak and live my truth, I was lost and had already lost.

Although we always want to be open to new relationships, it's also important to be savvy about them as well. I don't recommend putting blinders on and expecting that everyone will be honest and trustworthy. We have to recognize when people lack integrity, and we need to have the courage to deal with these situations.

We're hardwired for empathy and connection. Unfortunately, there are only so many hours in a day and so many years in a life. We can't be all things to all people. If we are, we will be nothing to ourselves because we won't live our Soul Purpose. To maximize our health, fulfillment, and contribution, we must prioritize the time and energy we give to others.

This may mean limiting the time we spend with certain people, or in some cases eliminating some people from our lives altogether and loving them from a distance. This can feel painful. Just as focusing on our Soul Purpose maximizes economic production, so does focusing on specific relationships to maximize our social health and contribution.

As I've shared in some of my earlier books, I've found it useful to consider three general categories for how I invest my time with relationships:

These are the people you say yes to. They energize and uplift you. They bring value to your world, and you can bring value to their world. They are your advocates, confidants, and maybe even your cheerleaders. If you find some you want to do business with, great. Ideally, invest the majority of your time with these people.

FRIENDS

These are people with whom you enjoy spending time, but they're not close confidants. They may not drain your energy, but they don't necessarily inspire your vision or share your core values. They may just be fun to be around. Probably not the people to share your vision with or to do business with.

BUDDIES

These are the people you say no to because they don't want to support you. They may be opposed to your values or consistently bring drama or drain your energy. Ideally, minimize your time and interactions with them. Eliminate the drama. Reserve that time and space for the friends who will help you out, who want to see you succeed, and with whom you build energy. You don't have to try to change friendlies or blow up the relationship. Just don't spend unnecessary time with them. Because time with them is spent, not invested. Learn the power of a positive "no," and how to elegantly step away. Too often it is tempting to get trapped by the urge to help people who don't want to be helped, or to change someone's perspective, opinion, or relationship with you.

FRIENDLIES

At one time in my life, I was an instructor for an organization that met quarterly. The founder introduced me for the first time, and I wasn't sure who he was talking about. He told the crowd I owned all the skyscrapers in Utah, when the truth was, I owned 45 percent of a three-story building. He then announced that all the other instructors were my clients; I hadn't met half of them. The introduction went on and on. I finally came to the stage and said, "I am not sure who just got introduced, but I look forward to meeting them or being them one day."

After I finished my talk, I immediately went to this individual's room to confront him. He listened and apologized, so I felt much better. The next time he introduced me, a new set of lies began. The more time I spent around this organization, the more drained I felt. It became apparent that no matter how much effort I gave, this wasn't going to change. Sure, he was a master at diffusing the situation, but I saw no evidence of intent to change. My life improved by simply removing myself from the organization. I took that energy and applied it to other organizations, including my own. Years later when I saw him, I kept it "friendly." He invited me back and I politely declined, effectively reclaiming my time.

From Lone Wolf to Visionary Pack

Jim Speer had been operating as an independent contractor for almost fifty years when he came to Wealth Factory in 2016. He wanted to scale and build something that would outlive him without borrowing money but had hit a wall. A one-man idea factory, he wanted to spend time on vision, but was trapped in operations and sales. He was playing to win, working sixty- to seventy-hour weeks. Though he enjoyed what he did, he hated getting stuck in details; and as a solo operator, too many details were limiting his potential. Kathy, his wife, hated his lack of order and didn't want to be working in the business, but she couldn't step away. The situation created marital stress.

They barely met the criteria for the program they wanted to join, but we liked their commitment and desire. We could see Jim was a hard worker but was missing Win, Then Play. Their company had focused on one small segment of a sixty-million-person market in the US; they were reaching only 4 percent of their potential customers. There was opportunity to branch out. For Jim, this was about building a team and letting go of activities he didn't want to be doing. These included:

> **OPERATIONS.** He hired a COO, a systems and operations person to keep things in order and free up Jim's time.

> **BOOKKEEPING AND FINANCIALS.** He hired a CFO who makes sure things are in proper order.

> **SALES.** He hired a sales manager who is hitting home runs and leveling up.

> **MARKETING.** Wealth Factory introduced him to a digital marketing firm.

No longer working seventy hours a week, Jim moved from surviving to thriving. Instead of drowning in details, he distributes these responsibilities to his team. He gets to spend time dreaming, creating, and building his vision. He sleeps better than ever and is energized to get up and work each morning.

Even better, Kathy is mostly out of the business and is only responsible for keeping the corporate books in order. She can be a grandma and live her life. Many of their relationship issues have been resolved.

His two sons are now in the business. They have options for the future, whether they wish to run it after Jim's retirement, or build it to sell. Right now, it looks like they want to run it. Jim's greatest pleasure is watching it grow and seeing his family succeed. With an abundance of cash flow, Jim is able to think beyond survival and has been focusing on legacy—investing in his heirs, creating experiences, writing family mission statements, and even designing a family crest.

Think it's too late for you? Jim is in his mid-seventies.

Many people come to me simply wanting the systems and structures to create financial freedom and independence. But they find that the real transformation happens when they shift their attention to discovering and working on their Soul Purpose.

Tips, Tricks, and Tactics to Reclaim Time

The world is relentless when it comes to demanding time. There is so much to do and so much to see, but no matter how hard you try, there is an infinite number of things to do—so many possibilities. Why is "no" so hard?

Is it because we are afraid of our own rejection, and we figure if we play the game of yes, people will reciprocate? Are we afraid of boredom and what our own thoughts may be? Are we afraid we are going to miss out on something? Or does it go back to the scarcity of there is only so much to go around so you have to take what you can?

When busyness occupies the mind, the imagination is trapped and vision is limited. Feeling the pull to always be doing something or going somewhere prevents us from being present. So here are a few things to consider that may allow you to recapture those moments: the gift of being present.

EMAIL MANAGEMENT: Do you love email? As my friend Dan Martell says, it is a public to-do list that is hard to control, unless you choose not to use it any longer. The less you email, the less email you get. You could use agendas and have anything that isn't urgent addressed in a weekly meeting by having someone monitor email for you. I eventually delegated and gave my email to others to manage.

SOCIAL MEDIA MANAGEMENT: Do you love social media? Does it fulfill you? Think about what you really want and why you want it. Create your own rules. What are you willing to do and not willing to do? What platforms matter to you? Or do you prefer to eliminate them all? Simply ask, does this bring happiness or distraction? What else could I do with the time?

I DELETED ALL APPS FROM MY PHONE BUT CAN POST FROM MY COMPUTER. I answer YouTube comments by filming videos. That is my path; what is yours? Create your rules and take back your life.

LIFE MANAGEMENT: There are people I want to create space for, invest time with. There is space in my calendar for date nights, hikes, rehearsals, and other items on a recurring basis. By being intentional, my calendar reflects what is most important in my life, including space for free time. Find your rhythms and protect them in your calendar. What rituals matter on a daily basis, or what traditions are your favorite that you can block out in advance? I have the flexibility to start meetings later in the day so I can have coffee with my wife, meditate, work out, and write. Does your calendar reflect how you want to live? Who you want to be?

OUTSOURCING: Do an inventory of your time and activities. What takes the most time and energy but provides the least fulfillment? Could you hire someone or work with an independent contractor part time as you build momentum?

For those who are not in a financial situation to implement any of these tips or tricks to reclaim time: revisit your win, eliminate escapism, ask for support, and invest in yourself. As you build momentum, as you have personal and professional profitability, then you can buy back your time. And you can delegate.

The rules and boundaries you don't create invite the world to decide for you (email, social media, apps, activities, etc.). And the world and society have an insatiable appetite for consumption. Until you know your value and define your win, there will never be enough time. When you know you *are enough* and are done with the chaos and drama, you will have more than enough time to build a life you love.

So know your win, know your rules, and live life on your terms. Invest in yourself, your lifestyle. Then continually blur the lines between work and play.

Reclaim Cash

"Mo Money Mo Problems"

—THE NOTORIOUS B.I.G. FT. PUFF DADDY

Net worth is often touted as the greatest indicator of wealth. Well, often people sacrifice their quality of life and delay happiness in order to chase net worth. There is a lot of advice out there telling people to delay gratification—to scrimp, save, and budget. But what happens when that advice is in direct opposition to your vision, to investing in yourself, and having a great quality of life?

You can save and accumulate net worth, but once you've built net worth, how do you access and utilize it? What matters most isn't how much money you save. Rather, it's how much Mental and Relationship Capital you create along the way, the memories you have, and your enjoyment of life without money being the reason or excuse you would do or not do something. Creating economic independence through cash flow is the Win, Then Play methodology, not slowly accumulating net worth.

Economic independence is when you have enough recurring revenue (aka cash flow) to cover your basic expenses from your assets. It is when income comes in even if you aren't working that day. It doesn't mean that income is completely passive, because you still monitor it and manage it to maintain it.

When you are economically independent, you have more choice, more freedom.

When you create economic independence, you will still build net worth, but it will be a by-product of your life, your value, and of your cash flow. Cash flow will also protect your net worth because you won't have to liquidate assets to pay the bills in economic downturn or turmoil.

Cash flow can be created by tapping into your Mental and Relationship Capital through building businesses, or investing in tangible and intangible assets, such as real estate or intellectual property, anything that can produce ongoing income.

Net Worth Is Not Your Worth

Retirement planning often focuses on net worth and neglects cash flow. The retirement goal is to build up enough of a nest egg to live on. The focus is on *possible* future growth, not optimizing current cash flow. As a result, net worth and retirement planning can be at odds with investing in you, growing your income, or improving your quality of life along the way.

People are trained, taught, and indoctrinated to set it and forget it (money) and to invest early, often, and always. To invest for the long haul . . . and it is just that, a haul. This is diametrically opposed to Win, Then Play. Retirement, net worth, and accumulation place value in a future number at the expense of your life today.

Where is the accountability, the joy? How will you know if it works? It requires contribution (setting money aside) at the cost of your contribution (your value and impact) because it is about funding someone else's dream before your own.

When you focus on cash flow each step of the way, you take control of your daily life. You gain control with each additional dollar that comes in on a recurring basis, month by month. That dollar is a vote for you to do more of what you really want without money tugging at your time or requiring as much of your energy or attention.

There is additional benefit to cash flow because it creates

space. When your expenses are handled from recurring revenue, you have options. When you take part of what you earn to build net worth, the next bill is paid from your labor rather than your assets' offspring (aka cash flow babies, aka cash money, aka cash dollars).

Trying to invest 10 percent into a retirement plan can be tough, especially when inflation is on the rise. Hoping for a 10 percent return can be even more uncertain and less likely. Instead, what if you had all your expenses handled by assets creating cash flow. Then all of your active income can build more assets, more quality of life, or allow you to do whatever you would like.

When my one-on-one immersion clients Clarke and April got out of the market in May of 2022, their advisor at the time told them, "This will be your biggest mistake—ever!" When I heard this, I imagined the guy stomping his foot like Veruca Salt in *Charlie and the Chocolate Factory*. He had a lot of nerve—especially since he lost Clarke and April's $600,000. Yes, you read that right. Even though they had millions to invest, their advisor told them to finance their house and put nearly all their cash out into the stock and bond market—because that's where he got paid. Clarke and April soon found themselves asset-rich and cash flow-poor, which meant they worried. All. The. Time. They worried because they didn't have influence over their retirement income. I'd be worried too.

What Clarke and April needed was a plan in alignment with their Investor DNA. I talk about this in detail in my books *Disrupting Sacred Cows* and *Budgeting Sucks*. Simply put, Investor DNA is how we relate to an investment. It is how we can be a better investor. Again, knowing yourself—your core values, the things that drive you (things that you are interested in and passionate about), plus your core competencies—these are the components of your Investor DNA. When we are aware of our Investor DNA, we can relate those qualities to the investments we make.

To live without dipping into their savings, Clarke and April needed $50,000 a month in cash flow, and they needed to invest in a way that provided inflation protection in things they understood. After one day, we found $32,000 a month in cash flow from great choices Clarke and April had made along the way. Some provided immediate cash flow because of properties they already owned or came from ingredients to fund and find the rest.

You may be at a different place in your life. Take away a zero or two or maybe add one or two. The key is in the philosophy and in the game you choose to play, knowing your Investor DNA.

$$\text{Mental Capital} \times \text{Relationship Capital} = \text{Financial Capital}$$

Unfortunately, with retirement planning, "investing" and "stocks" are basically synonymous. Many people don't even realize the variety of investment options they have—financial and otherwise. They ask for stocks instead of looking for investments they can use to create value and cash flow.

The Conservative has an accumulation mindset and sets aside money hoping it will increase over time through compound interest. Most people think compound interest is a miracle. I share a lot about this in my book *Killing Sacred Cows*. For now, I'll just say that I think it's a miracle that people believe compound interest is a miracle. Accumulation is the opposite of Win, Then Play. It's slow, risky, and it doesn't work in the long run.

Believing in accumulation (aka net worth) is to believe that money is power. Instead, learn to put faith in the things that *create* money, not money itself. Money isn't manifested and exchanged until value is created. Remember, value is in the eye of the beholder. You—your perspective, your fulfillment, your desires—determine value. It's only an expression of value creation, which comes from you. Remember your Value Index, the number you came up with in chapter 1. This is the number where you stop thinking about getting to a specific number and start thinking about the value you would create. Focusing on your Value Index frees you from an accumulation mindset.

The more we set money aside in investments we don't understand, for a payoff in the far-off future, the more risk we take. So, before saving a penny more, before taking any risk with your money, let's find ways to save you money and improve your cash flow without cutting back.

Boost Your Bottom Line and Plug Leaks

When it comes to expenses, the standard advice we're often given is to cut, cut, cut. Scrimp, sacrifice, and save. **However, no one shrinks their way to wealth, no matter what the Miser says.** Some expenses you will want to eliminate, but others are best to manage, address, and even increase.

Those stuck Playing Not to Lose overemphasize budgeting.

Budgeting sucks. That's why hardly anyone sticks to it. It implies restraint and sacrifice, rather than abundance. It means reduction and selfishness rather than production and cooperation.

Budgeting ignores details and nuances that create wealth. It tends to invite scarcity thinking. Budgeting is about eliminating experiences, or not taking trips, or even delaying making memories. However, for a business owner, high-income earner, or someone already making more than they spend, carrying that advice too far leads straight into Playing Not to Lose. The obsession of budgeting occupies the mind, prevents more productive thoughts, and limits value.

You can't scrimp your way to happiness. Being a cheapskate isn't fun. And it can really impact the people you love most, where they feel you love money over them. What good is planning for a future when you let your actual present slip away? To make matters worse, when you die after living like the Miser, your heirs are likely to blow the money in a few years. Creating a life you love is unlikely if you never enjoy your money or create meaningful experiences.

Budgeting has come to mean *can't*:

> I *can't* afford it.
> *I can't* do date night.
> *I can't* arrange that trip with the family.
> *I can't* hire help; to save money, I have to do everything myself.

In truth, there's a much smarter way, one that will free up *way* more cash than clipping coupons. After reviewing people's finances over the past twenty years, I have found over 10 percent of their income is lost through unnecessary taxes, interest, insurance, and investment fees. By structuring each of these properly, thousands of people have saved thousands of dollars per month—without changing their daily spending habits.

In *Killing Sacred Cows*, my first book, I illustrate how small fees have a big impact on long-term performance and how to detect and eliminate nonperforming fees. In *Budgeting Sucks* I unveil Cash Flow Optimization and all the ways you can reduce your interest rates with the 3Rs: renegotiate, restructure, and reallocate. And in *What Would the Rockefellers Do?* I lay out how to properly structure insurance in order to avoid duplicate coverages, identify improper structure, and properly transfer risk. You can go to my YouTube channel at Garrett.live or YouTube.com/garrettgundersontv to learn, and sometimes laugh, to find all the different ways to keep more of what you make. This includes my tax frameworks. Because you know what is funny about tax? NOTHING.

So, stop by **Garrett.live**, free of charge, to legally, and ethically, stop tipping the government and keep more of your cash. You are welcome!

Be Conscious with Your Money

Mindful Cash Management is a methodology where you don't track your expenses down to the last penny; instead you prioritize to get the most out of your spending. You're simply aware of how much money is flowing through your hands at any given time, by automating how you save money.

Mindful Cash Management is making sure you are aware of your expenses but not held captive by them. The process involves tracking your expenses and cash flow on a weekly or biweekly basis. You simply know what you are spending, avoid spending more than you make, and leave room to spend on things you value. No reason to devote countless hours constraining, as long as you don't spend more than you make and pay yourself first.

This structure invites the concept of abundance into your perspective on money. It comes from asking yourself what it is that brings you joy, fulfillment, and utility. It's not about what others think you should do. It is about allocating money on your terms.

Mindful Cash Management begins with understanding what's happening with your finances and being more accountable with your money. Over the next thirty days, look at your expenses and categorize your spending into one of these four expense categories:

> Destructive: Expenses that limit your human life value, cause you to go into debt, or go unused. So, money you spend on addictions or destructive vices. Overdraft and late fees, and fines. Borrowing to consume "extras" (stuff you don't really need) and experiences, such as a vacation you really can't afford.

> Lifestyle: Expenses that allow you to enjoy life now by spending money on things you value. These expenses can be fun and create memories, but they don't directly build assets or income. They include things like clothing, entertainment subscriptions, cell phones, din-

ing out, event tickets, and vacations. The key is to pay cash and never borrow to consume.

> Protective: Expenses that manage your risk and protect you and your property from damage and loss. So, insurance, including life, disability, health, auto, liability, and others. Also, liquid savings, estate planning, asset protection, and emergency preparedness.

> Productive: Expenses that enhance your life now and in the future. They are assets that produce more than the liability. These expenses may include purchasing a rental property or a business. If you already own a business, productive expenses may include hiring a new employee, or investing in marketing, training, or time-saving equipment.

I'd like to share a few ways it can make sense to increase productive expenses. I put recording studios in my house and my cabin so I could do quality videos for YouTube and so my Zoom meetings look much better. When I sold Wealth Factory, the organization started spending twice as much on ads through YouTube, Facebook, and Google, increasing their reach and profit without me being on a single stage. By hiring my project manager, Tricia Fogg, I am confident the details of my business are being handled. She keeps me on track with my calendar and deadlines, which massively increases my capacity, energy, and enjoyment in what I do.

Simply follow this recipe:

1. **ELIMINATE** destructive expenses.

2. **MANAGE** lifestyle expenses by paying cash for these purchases. (Potential exception: auto and home loans.)

3. **ADDRESS** protective expenses and maximize their efficiency to get the most bang for your buck.

4. **INCREASE** productive expenses—if they are still productive and you can manage their growth.

Build a Solid Foundation

Part of keeping more of your cash is having a solid foundation to prevent money leaks and losses. How do you know if have a healthy baseline for financial security? First, answer the following questions:

1. **HAVE** you transferred catastrophic risks through proper insurance, corporate structure, estate planning, and asset protection?

2. **HAVE** you built up at least six months of liquidity?

3. **HAVE** you utilized risk mitigation techniques to protect your downside by adding collateral, obtaining personal guarantees, or putting stop-losses on your investments?

If you can say yes to the questions above, you're in pretty good shape. Now consider the next questions:

1. **DO** you have to pay double-digit rates to borrow funds?

2. **DO** you have to borrow to consume?

3. **DO** your investments create worry and scarcity thinking due to volatility or not fully understanding how your money works?

4. **DO** you pay yourself last?

This is all part of a practical application to support peace of mind, clarity, and build financial confidence so you can build and live the life you love.

The Love Movement

"He said, 'You become. It takes a long time. That's why it doesn't happen often to people who break easily, or have sharp edges, or who have to be carefully kept. Generally, by the time you are Real, most of your hair has been loved off, and your eyes drop out and you get loose in the joints and very shabby. But these things don't matter at all, because once you are Real you can't be ugly, except to people who don't understand.'"

— THE VELVETEEN RABBIT

What's your number? The number where you stop thinking about how you'd spend your money and start thinking about service, about what lights you up? We've unmasked nearly all the reasons why you might let something get in the way of experiencing this life and work you imagined. Your Value Index vision takes a back seat when we think we don't have enough time or money, or even love. You've reclaimed time and recovered cash. Love is the fuel that powers your vision, and yet we have forgotten its power.

We live in a world divided.

My team versus your team.

My town versus your town.

My country versus your country.

My belief versus your belief.

Roe versus Wade.

Guns versus no guns.

Stand versus kneel.

Racism. Sexism. Ageism.

What you can say and what you can't say.

Which side are you on?

And what will it cost you to choose?

Can you feel the weight and pressure of trying to figure it all out and be perfect?

Do you know the right answer, and if you do, does that make others wrong or less lovable?

What if you were on the side of love?

Of listening.

Of seeing others and allowing yourself to be seen? The real you.

What if the real answer to all of this came in the form of a question. One simple, yet powerful and profound question:

What would love do?

Not what would I do for money, but how would love show up? Beginning with love for yourself.

What could you forgive yourself for and let go of?

No matter what the belief is or the circumstance, could we actually choose love? Show up with love. Be love.

Love is abundant, powerful, and the ultimate Win, Then Play.

No amount of mathematics can explain love.

No law can dictate how or whom you love; it is a personal, powerful choice.

We must remember love is a choice. In the face of all complexity and adversity, it is in our power to choose love.

It can be hard to love ourselves.

It can be even harder to be ourselves.

It is hard for me.

I grew up and live in Utah. I have never been Mormon, yet my father's side of the family comes from Mormon royalty aka Latter-Day Saints or LDS. My great-great-great grandfather was Wilford Woodruff, president of the LDS church. My partners I lost in the flight were even LDS. Hell, if you google me, one autofill is Garrett Gunderson Mormon. Also, Garrett Gunderson comedian? But it is hurtful that there is a question mark after comedian—ha!

This led to me being a chameleon for far too long in my life—blending in. Using my energy to keep track of how I should appear to fit in and bending to be who people wanted me to be at the expense of who I really am.

Is there human connection in that agreement to fall in line?

Yeah, suffering the future. Carrying the stress before it happens by trying to appease and do what I thought others wanted.

For example, I love to swear. But that isn't accepted in the culture of Utah. To this day I still have to release the worry that my early mentors will be disappointed or judge me if I swear. Also, I didn't drink in certain groups growing up. Or at events outside of my home state I would make sure to drink, so people would know I am from Utah, but not of Utah. Why?

Because I wanted to be accepted. Because I thought it was the sacrifice required to succeed. Sacrifice isn't just about hard work, it's about anything that prevents us from living our Soul Purpose or being present in the moment. I didn't know if I could be successful otherwise, so I'd sacrifice who I was for what I thought I wanted—to be admired, but even deeper, to be loved.

Sacrifice.

Sacrifice is a wolf in sheep's clothing. So subtle, so sneaky. Sacrifice is a word that so many people say and believe is required to succeed today. I sacrificed expression and created constant stress in my life simply to be accepted.

Societal acceptance. Who determines what is acceptable? The woke? The government? Corporations? These ideas have been tried for millennia and have failed. The ideas that money is power, that it takes money to make money, that you have to sacrifice to succeed, take what you can, get what is yours, that zero-sum game of scarcity that reduces your life to a number—suddenly your moments are lost to a false promise of security provided by a government or corporation.

Society is great at giving an example of what not to be. What not to do. But I had bought in. I chased the trophies and the net worth. I did what I was told, at the expense of my life, my vision, and my winning game. I went through much of my life as a people pleaser worried about others' thoughts at the expense of my own expression, which created chronic worry—worry handed down for generations. This worry misled me to think I couldn't have a direct conversation with someone because it could hurt someone else's feelings and that was somehow more important than me or my feelings.

The errant belief that told me to avoid conflict and enjoy life—not so easy. That energy gets drained, my thoughts were never free. By avoiding I ended up conflicted.

The key is to come from compassion and to listen.

To understand.

To show up with love.

Rather than condemn someone else who has a different belief, learn from them, and simply go back to the question, What would love do?

When I was eighteen years old I spent the summer in South Korea. My friend said I could make money modeling. Funny, I'm six foot three and white, not sure why I thought that would work. I taught English instead.

Traveling abroad opened my eyes. I thought America was the only free country, but it didn't seem any less free in Seoul, South Korea. It is embarrassing to admit, but I thought that

Americans were superior, or even favored. Then I was introduced to an amazing culture and wonderful people. My perspective was limited—limited views about freedom, about the world, about a lot.

Where else was I set in my false beliefs and ways?

Perspectives become standards of judgment, labeling, and discriminating, destroying connection and creating division.

To put people into left or right, agree or disagree, gay or straight, right or wrong simply removes love. Even the fact that I am a wealthy white man writing this may trigger judgment because of how much less severe my situation or circumstance is due to my privilege. I'm aware.

Our environment matters. I know I am lucky, but all I have is not due solely to luck. It is in the work, but not the hustle and grind type. The work in loving myself enough to live my Soul Purpose and having the hard conversations to stay connected. Overcoming fear, letting go of anger, and discovering who we are is the hardest work, but it's worth the effort.

I have amazing parents who love me and an amazing family that supports me. And we don't agree on everything, either. Mask or no mask. Vaccination or no vaccination. These are issues that required tough conversations to stay connected. It wasn't easy, but we found the core values we shared—protecting those we love. Even if we didn't see the process the same, we could agree that we wanted what was best for each other.

Censorship is not the answer. Censorship eventually amplifies the problem and increases resentment, judgment, and division. Feeling that we aren't allowed to feel or speak up because our problems are small compared to others' traps our emotions and governs our future actions, which leads to staying small-minded. These unspoken thoughts begin to fester until we search for a group that feels similar to us. But what if that tribe also feels unheard, angry, and builds momentum through resentment and exclusion? What if fear becomes the fuel? Where is the love, where is the win?

Fuck being forced to choose a side and be ousted due to the color of your skin, sexual preference, or political stance. It is time to love.

To accept all that we are and have to offer.

To stand for our quality of life individually as an example, rather than fall into the trap of dividing and simplistically relegating people into categories and beliefs.

To discover our inner artist.

To stand up to the tyranny and oppression of being valued according to our bank account or social media status.

Love doesn't require you to agree or behave in a way that fits anyone's control fantasy. You aren't a character in their book losing a sense of who you are to simply appease them or earn their approval.

Conditional love is a mistake. Chasing that love while losing who you are is the mistake. That narrative of being loved for what you do more than who you are creates the losing games and is a counterfeit of love, fueled by censorship. That lie says you are your accomplishments and mistakes, rather than truth, that you are love.

Live a life you love, learn from your mistakes, take responsibility, and know your mistakes don't make you less loveable; they make you human. Let go of blame and resentment to awaken to the fullness of who you are—a creative and loving being, worthy of love and full of value.

Let go of the hurt and leave behind the stories of doubt, fear, and worry. There is nothing to prove.

KNOW YOU ARE LOVED.

KNOW YOU ARE VALUABLE.

KNOW YOU ARE ENOUGH.

There is nothing to do and nowhere to be, but here, now. In love.

I love you.

AND:

If you are wondering where I stand on the issues listed to start this chapter, I stand for people, for humanity, and for the love that unites us all.

}

EXERCISE:

Love in Action

WRITE A LOVE LETTER TO YOURSELF.

> Start by listing what you don't like about yourself. Jot down all your mistakes, perceived flaws, and issues.

> Then, find gratitude for each one of your mistakes, flaws, and issues. Note how these aspects of yourself have been useful to you. What if the things you're afraid to admit were designed to help you appreciate duality, to experience life?

What if they are not to be ignored or hidden, but to be held to the light and to be felt fully?

› Now write down the things about yourself that make you proud. Think beyond winning awards and achieving goals for success. Include moments of kindness and generosity. Jot down stuff you've made, or problems you've solved, or ideas you've come up with. Note the times you showed up as your best self, or stayed the course when things got hard, or found the courage to do something terrifying. Pay special attention to the private wins, the moments you're proud of that no one knows about.

› Next, replace the word "proud" with the word "love."

› Draft the letter, noting all the gifts and insights from your flaws, mistakes, and issues. Add all the other reasons why you love yourself (from #3).

› Now, send a love letter to your five-year-old self. Be playful, thankful, and let that child know you are okay, you've got this, and you have made it this far.

› Finally, send a love letter to the person you will be on your death bed. Write into existence who you are committed to being, what you want to be remembered and acknowledged for.

› Read your letters to yourself (every month).

EXERCISE:

*Write a Love Letter
to Someone Else*

If you aren't ready to write a love letter to yourself, write one to someone else. I have a habit of sending handwritten notes and letters of love and gratitude to people every week. It helps me to stay in the power of love and gratitude. I'm also lucky that many people send love notes to me as well, perhaps because my notes give them permission to express themselves. Here are some ideas:

> Send a love letter to someone who would least expect it.

> Send a love letter to someone who rarely gets thanks for the work they do.

> Send a love letter to someone who you haven't talked to in a long time, someone you want to reconnect with.

> Send a love letter to someone who always remembers your birthday.

> Send a love letter to your significant other.

> Send a love letter to your kids, even if they are too young to read it.

> Send a love letter to someone you're estranged from.

> Send a love letter to someone who doesn't realize how they've helped you.

Self-Love Fuels Your Vision

Realize that anything you can see and acknowledge in someone else is something you have within. The gratitude is a mirror of what you have as well. Know you are loved. Know you are valuable. And know the best way to create value and to win comes from a place of love.

When you are afraid to be vulnerable and ask for help, it's a sign that you may not feel worthy and that you may not fully act in loving ways toward yourself. And as long as you continue to believe this, your Value Index vision will be just out of reach. How can we be fully abundant if we don't accept ourselves, in all our glory and imperfections?

When we don't accept ourselves, we limit the love for ourselves and others.

When we don't trust ourselves, we limit the love for ourselves and others.

When we compete with others, we limit the love for ourselves and others.

The Play to Win competition creates fear, fights, and distractions. Why do we want to win at another's expense? To survive? Or is it to prove our value? It's not a fight, and the only way we lose is in the absence of love, not knowing how lovable we are. When we allow our pain or fear to diminish our value, our vision, or hide our Soul Purpose, we lose.

Rather than work to gain admiration, realize the admiration we seek is within. How we are loved, first and foremost by ourselves—that is the question. Just like there is no money manual we are handed with our first dollar, we aren't given a step-by-step process the first time we don't feel lovable.

Win, Then Play is when there is nothing to get, and nothing

to get to or get away from. You don't have to hate what you do now to have a life you enjoy later. Constantly looking for someone else's story, rather than creating your own, limits vision and cultivates jealousy.

Self-love fuels your vision. It's the missing link. The holy grail. The turbo-charge you need to make all your impossible dreams a reality.

Love is your win.

When you choose love, you have already won.

When John Lennon was five years old, his mother told him, "Happiness is the key to life." Later, when he went to school, his teacher asked the class to write down what they wanted to be when they grew up. Lennon's homework read: "Happy." When his teacher read it, he told Lennon he must not have understood the assignment.

Lennon replied, "You don't understand life."[2]

You get it. You understand the game of life, a life of honoring yourself and creating value. And yet you have one vital step left to take: love.

If happiness is the key to life, the ultimate Win, Then Play, then *love* is the key to happiness.

Love for your ideas, and interests, and vision.

Love for others.

And especially, love for yourself.

---

2 "John Lennon, Quotes," Goodreads.com, accessed September 13, 2022, https://www.goodreads.com/author/quotes/19968.John_Lennon.

"Your vision will become clear only when you can look into your own heart. Who looks outside, dreams; who looks inside, awakes."

—CARL JUNG

CHAPTER

An Extraordinary Life

"May today there be peace within. May you trust that you are exactly where you are meant to be. May you not forget the infinite possibilities that are born of faith in yourself and others. May you use the gifts that you have received, and pass on the love that has been given to you. May you be content with yourself just the way you are. Let this knowledge settle into your bones, and allow your soul the freedom to sing, dance, praise, and love. It is there for each and every one of us."

—ST. THÉRÈSE

C hasing money cost me.

Greed misled me.

And yet the world applauded, leaving me unfulfilled.

It started early for me. At age fifteen I started a car detailing business: Garrett Gunderson's Car Care. With this business I won $5,000 for being the Governor's Young Entrepreneur of the year, which led me to a career in financial services at the age of nineteen. I was looking for a way to invest my $5,000 and was offered an internship with a New York City–based insurance and investment firm.

From this early age I made money because, well, money was my priority, my obsession. And candidly, there could never be enough. Even when I achieved a financial goal, there was no time to celebrate. No matter what I was doing, or how much I had accomplished, I harshly judged myself for not doing better because there was always someone else with more. I thought I could always work harder, do more, and ultimately have more.

Play to win.

When people asked me about my hobbies, for years my answer was, "Hobbies? What do you mean? I run a business; that is my hobby. I invest money; that is my hobby." I was so addicted to work because I wanted to be accomplished, wealthy, and this left little room for anything, or anyone, else.

Having money at an early age created a false confidence because of "perceived" success. But with an inflated ego came risk and self-deception. For example, not knowing the difference between luck and skill. My first real estate deals were lucrative, but that was due to timing, not knowledge. This led to buying more and more, even spending an entire vacation working with attorneys and bankers to close a deal while my wife sat alone. It was a losing game.

Before I understood Investor DNA, I remember hearing and repeating, "You should buy real estate; everyone wealthy does." A friend who invested in real estate even planted the seed for me to start a hard money-lending fund to support real estate investors. He said, "Hey, you are already referring people to others. Why not start your own fund to make more and actually get paid?"

I couldn't think about anything else for weeks, so I started one without realizing some important, essential aspects of money management.

Money allocation takes up space in the mind, and lots of energy is required. So, saying yes to this so-called opportunity meant I said no to other things. And with each new idea, each new venture, I said no to my family, my health, my personal fulfillment, and unbeknownst to me, my impact.

When it comes to money, some decide to play not to lose, thinking there is too much to know, it is too hard to handle, and they shirk responsibility by handing over their money every month to so-called experts. They fund retirement plans with mutual funds they know little about and hope it will all grow.

Others, like me, decide there is never enough and go for more. But it begs the question: At what cost? Why was *more* always my answer?

I could never have admitted it at the time, but money defined me. It isn't easy to admit this now.

I thought my self-worth was the same as my net worth. I was young and had a goal to be worth millions before I was thirty. Yes, then I could finally be proud, then I could prove I was worth something. But no matter how much I made, there would still be an emptiness inside.

No amount of money could fill the void where I didn't love or accept myself.

More isn't a pathway to love, more isn't a winnable game. More is a moving target: more money, more achievements, more opportunity.

My misguided definition of success informed my actions. It impacted every aspect of my life, and of the lives of those I love. More is a seductress, with attractive returns and accolades, but the costs are rarely understood.

My philosophy created an unwinnable game; emphasizing more over better, quantity not quality, and net worth took priority over peace of mind or being present.

I chased money because I thought it was power. Well, more than that, I thought it was value. My value. Yeah, not just a representation of the value I created, but my actual value and worth. And the game of more, my pursuit of money, prevented me from experiencing, expressing, and accepting what I already had, what I truly desired.

To love and be loved.

But playing to win leaves little room for love and happiness. The tireless pursuit of more left me tired. My reward: exhaustion.

There is no lasting win in the Consumer Condition. There was no number that would matter or get me to love myself or enjoy my life in a losing game. I didn't see that. I couldn't see that. I was pursuing net worth, well, until I added a zero, until my business partner Les McGuire asked, "What's your number?"

Each time I added a zero, my view opened up more. Finally, as the numbers got beyond what I could spend, a sense of calm came over me. It was a knowing, a state of being and shift that transformed my life and perspective forever. Why would I wait for an amount of money to determine my daily actions, my Soul Purpose? *If . . . then . . . when. Eventually. Sacrifice.* These are all terms that mislead. But by doing today what I would do in the future once I hit those numbers, I would be set free immediately.

I could finally see that my actual number **was no number at all.**

It was this simple yet profound exercise that gave me my freedom. Knowing what I would do with a million dollars a month was daunting in the world of status but liberating in the world of impact. With financial independence, there is permission to do what I truly enjoy, what really speaks to me, and what I would want to do on a daily basis. Even though it was an exercise, it immediately impacted my day-to-day decisions.

Financial freedom can happen in a moment; it is a choice.

When money is no longer our primary reason or excuse for doing or not doing something, you win, you are free. The What's Your Number? exercise was an immediate shift, transforming my mindset.

It was time to redefine my life and let go of what was no longer in my highest and best interest.

If money were of no concern, most real estate wouldn't make my list. I didn't love real estate. I wasn't excited to invest in oil and gas or IPOs. These led me away from what I loved. I love building relationships through entertaining and comedy.

Yet, my schedule showed a different story: meetings with bankers, attorneys, accountants—nothing funny there.

I immediately changed my schedule. I started dating my wife. I created a guys' night out weekly with my boys. I started to delegate, and with the found time I learned to fly-fish, hired a barista to show me how to make the perfect latte, and started playing guitar again. I wrote every day: jokes, poems, books, and even a one-man show.

I found time to take walks, tinker around my cabin, and meditate.

This is legacy, living it first by investing time with my family.

The game of more didn't lead to abundance, self-care, or connection. The number doesn't matter, but the question does.

Again, if money were of no concern, what would you do?

It was time to allow my Soul Purpose to guide me, my intuition, my inner voice. This was my path to fulfillment and impact.

Even though I put my quality of life and Soul Purpose as the priority, my impact grew.

We don't always know our impact in the moment, but when it is an extension of a life well lived, the expression of who we are when we are at our best, we win, and so do others.

I experienced my impact when fellow financial revolutionary Caleb Guilliams gave me a gift. He asked me to keynote his event. With short notice and a busy schedule, at first I was inclined to decline the invitation, but I took a moment and listened to my intuition, that inner voice, and said yes.

Caleb gathered a group of financial leaders, agents, planners, and educators with exceptional processes and platforms.

In a packed room, he brought me to the front and asked the crowd, "Who has read Garrett's books?" Every hand went up.

He then asked, "Whose life has been changed by this man?" The crowd stood up and clapped.

What? It was profound. I had no clue. I was moved to tears.

For the next hour and a half, I shared my soul. I shared *this* story, and we connected.

The messages I shared that day: be abundant and collaborate. In Win, Then Play, mistakes don't define you; we all make mistakes. Money is a by-product of value but is not why you are valuable. When you create a life of love and value, you win.

That experience nourished my soul, elevated my energy, and inspired me. I added value to them, and then the value was returned.

Two mentors of mine from the early 2000s were in the room. I was able to acknowledge them, hug them, and tell them how much they have meant to me, and then they shared a similar sentiment of appreciation.

The rest of the day I signed books, but more importantly, I was present with people. We had permission to be vulnerable. Connecting is more profound than conversation. It is sharing all we are, the glory and the imperfections. It is listening. Creating a space for others to share.

Throughout the day, the conversations and stories attendees shared caught me by surprise. Stories of how my videos, books, and example had shifted careers, mindsets, and improved their lives. And others opened up and shared their despair, processing deep emotions previously bottled up, because I shared how I stopped letting money rule my life and chose Soul Purpose instead.

I discovered that taking care of myself, my family, and doing deep personal work and choosing expression over perfection lifted others. It wasn't about counting the likes or social media shares; it was about being the best of who I am.

It wasn't the awards or accolades, and the attendees that day didn't even know my net worth. They had never seen my home or my car. I used those status symbols to prove my value early in my career. Often those come from competition and separation, but they're never as fulfilling as connection and collaboration.

Chasing money didn't provide connection, only obsession and depression. So, redefine investing. Invest in your winning game and those that help you play it.

Find your co-creator, and invest in relationships that support and inspire you. You don't have to do this by yourself. Even if you don't have money, use the currency of connection. Be open, vulnerable, and real. Remember this when life is difficult, when we make mistakes, or feel out of flow. Be open, vulnerable, and real.

Pretending doesn't help anyone; it prolongs the process.

We give permission to others when we open up, when we really share and ask for support. Often when we struggle on our own, we rob people of their value, of our presence and the gift of connection.

All these difficult moments I am sharing led to being able to lead the group of "competitors" that day. But they were really co-creators, collaborators. By giving my best, they returned the favor.

When we view ourselves from the perspective of scarcity, the Shadow Personas control our actions; they trap us and destroy our value. Playing to win led to racing for more yet limited my impact and vision. The simple What's Your Number? exercise was the key to breaking free. Now, I was able to have a greater impact by creating and living a life I love: finding ways to create value from my Winning Persona, with a vision that compels me each and every day, while asking for support along the way.

It is your turn, your time now.

You now have all the insights and tools you need to build a life you love. Your Value Index will guide you, and your Winning Personas will help you build any dream. You've uncovered Hidden Capital and you now understand the Cycle of Creation, so you can launch your purpose-driven product or service. You know how to recover money and time, letting go of the decisions and commitments you made when living by your Shadow Personas. And all this empowers you to play a different game— to Win, Then Play.

You're not the same person you were when you started reading this book. What will you do with these strategies? Your newfound knowledge? What impact could *you* have simply by doing what you are called to do, doing what interests you, doing what gives you joy?

Your win has nothing to do with Wall Street, or retirement accounts, or picking the right investment. What's Your Number? is about living your life from abundance. Even if you are struggling to make ends meet, be more resourceful. Tap into your Hidden Capital, that Relationship Capital. Ask for support.

You are not alone.

It is time. Time to create space for you. Find your flow.

FIND a hobby that is just for you. It has nothing to do with money and everything to do with caring for yourself.

WRITE a love letter. If you can write one to yourself, that is great. If you aren't ready, find someone you can unconditionally love and write them a letter, letting them know how much you care. By pouring love into someone else, you're looking at all you admire in them. You can only see in others what you have in yourself.

ASK each day, "What's my win? What is one step that will allow me to begin now?" Perfectly imperfect. Progress over perfection. Just one step.

An extraordinary life awaits and depends on it.

One from humility.

One from love.

I love you.

A Gift for You

My Grandpa Gunderson used to take me fishing as a kid. We would troll out on his boat and catch dozens of fish. It felt easy. It was fun. When we got back to camp, I would take the same fishing equipment and try to catch some more on the river by myself. But no matter how long I tried, no matter how focused I was, I never caught a thing. Fishing a river is very different than fishing from a boat. But as a kid, I didn't know that. I just wanted to show my grandpa I could catch fish on my own.

Hard work with the wrong philosophy leads to frustration. Often, we are economic toddlers trying to catch fish in the stream with equipment meant for the lake. No matter how hard we try, we will be disappointed. Trying to do everything on our own creates limitation. Making money and keeping money are different skill sets. Doing too much on our own leads to exhaustion. To win the game of money, it is essential to know you have a Money Persona that rules every financial decision you make.

Without knowing our Money Persona, we are more susceptible to conflict and chaos. We are all in store for financial surprises, but with the proper preparation, education, and collaboration, we can win.

To help you, I created the Money Persona Quiz. When you take this quiz, you'll get a free report that outlines your

Money Persona, illustrates what your best money traits are, and highlights danger spots to watch out for—all based upon your personality and circumstances. Simply go to moneyunmasked. com/quiz and you can take it for free. It's my gift to you—you don't even have to opt in to join my email list. Take the quiz to find out what your Money Persona is.

Destructive money triggers of your Shadow Persona can get you in deep financial trouble if you aren't aware of them. So take the quiz now and learn how to leverage your Winning Persona.

Acknowledgments

There is this myth of being self-made. There is no such thing as self-made. My life is co-created and possible because of the relationships, love, and support I receive.

To my favorite person in the world, my wife. Thanks for seeing my raw ingredients and loving me for all that I am, good and bad. I've been married twenty years, and for my wife, Carrie, this is like the twenty-third version of me. It has taken lots of discovery, personal work, and tough conversations to choose love over fear and become the more self-expressed version I am today. Carrie has been my rock, the love of my life, supporting me through it all. I wasn't always an extraordinary husband, but thanks to her patience and perseverance, we have created an extraordinary life together. As a glimpse into the type of woman she is, when I chose to pursue comedy, she wrote me a note that is more meaningful than any accolade or award: "Where you go, we go. Your dreams are our dreams. My wins are your wins. Together we walk, by each other's side. My home is wherever you are."

To my sons. I love being your dad. This book was written with you in my mind. I wanted to reach you, make an impact, and share the best of me with you. The Money Personas are a common part of our conversations now. The family pastime has become Mom telling stories of me being a Miser when we were first married so you both can laugh hysterically. One of my favorite things is when you tell me the characters' Money Persona on TV shows. You have shown me how to care and love in a way that wasn't possible without being your father. Thank you.

To my parents. As I have done extensive work with self-discovery, my mom always apologizes or feels bad for "messing me up"—ha! The thing is, no matter who you are, we all can use some healing. I couldn't have asked for better parents. My mom's laugh is why I love comedy; it just feels like love. My dad is hilarious and showed me how to connect through comedy. I always feel loved and knew and know I can count on you. All those countless times of getting me focused on school, activities, guitar, sports . . . it has paid off, and I want you to know I deeply love and appreciate you.

To those Catalysts, you are a special, wonderful gift. Catalysts are advocates and connectors that advance a relationship at least five years through their introduction. Rich Christiansen. Jeff Hays. John Ruhlin. Patrick Gentempo. Jon Butcher. Barry Katz. Marty Callner.

I even roped some Creators and Catalysts into doing some comedy with me during my debut fifteen-city tour: Garrett J. White, Derek Coburn, Yanik Silver, Scott Rowe, Brad Boeke, Jonathan Sprinkles, Peter Martone, Matt Hubbard, Ben Greenfield, and Ryan Moran. A special shout-out to Keith Yackey for joining me in multiple cities and bringing so much more joy and fun.

And those (co)Creators, who act like magnets, attracting and pulling the best out of me, thank you for making this book possible.

AJ Harper. You are such an articulate, amazing writer, and even better friend. Thanks for being THE key co-creator unleashing my writing skills and making this book possible. I just love you and am so grateful for you.

Michael Port, the director of my one-man show, *Already Won*. You bring this content to the stage by turning the Money Personas into characters. Michael, you are a deep well of wisdom, unlocking so much that I didn't know was there. Your brilliance has footprints throughout this book. Thank you.

Larry Moss. Thank you for noticing my ticks, my escapisms, so I can heal, be present, and bring words to life through performance. As I told you the very first time we met, I love you.

Mark "Marcus" Hardy. You gave me my shot at comedy. You were the first person I called when I was ready to do stand-up, and it changed my life forever. You have worked with me on jokes, books, videos, my comedy special, and pretty much every project. Life is more fun with laughter, and you, my friend, have brought that to me.

Dr. Craig Manning, a mentor and partner who gave me the knowledge and science to unlock hidden potential, create predictable results, and have sustained happiness.

Sally Hogshead. This book was born the day I did an immersion for you at the Wealth Factory office. You asked where you could read more about what I was sharing—nowhere, until now. Thanks for your vision, talent, and belief—here it is manifest.

Stephen Palmer. This book is only possible because of what we started so many years ago with *Killing Sacred Cows* and what you have done to dissect and discover these Money Personas—thank you.

Corey Wert, my partner, my friend. We win when we play, and I love to play the game of business and life with you. You have the key to unlock the content within. Thanks for your guidance and influence.

Ross Aubrey and Lindsay Stahl for supporting my comedy at a whole new level and introducing me to the world of NFTs so I can express myself through music and build community with fewer gatekeepers and more focus on value.

And thanks to all those Planners, which made any of this possible. There are so many moving pieces with a book, a business, and life; this is where the rubber meets the road.

Norm Westervelt. You have been my fierce protector, mentor, and implementor—thank you. Together we are better!

And the efficient, resourceful Mindful Managers.

Tricia Fogg. My sister. Always there for me. Taking care of anything and everything. One of the best parts of life is that I have you. You always have my back.

Teri Cochrane, what a gift to my family. Helping us with our health—physically and emotionally. You have changed my family's life forever.

And then there are the mirrors. The ones that reflect back to us and show us who we really are. Another shout-out to my wife, Carrie Gunderson, and to my dear friend Aaron Anderson. Thanks, brother.

Then there are the believers in all the good that people have to offer, from the time it was a seed within and the world was yet to know. You uplift us all with your encouragement, but most of all your love, the unconditional love not to be earned, but merely because we are inherently valuable.

To my irrational believers: Anna Mae Webb, James "Papa" Eaquinto, Jacquie Gunderson, Teri Tubbs, Dean Templin, Mark Barton, Sandra Lord, Steve Harrop, Les McGuire, Greg Barrick, Nancy Ogilvie, and Moe Abdou.

Index

About the Author

GARRETT is a modern-day "renaissance man." Well, maybe.

An Inc. 500 founder of a financial firm and amateur barista.

A rookie fly fisherman and *Wall Street Journal* #1 best-selling author.

A public speaker who's delivered hundreds of keynotes, and a mediocre guitar player at home.

A bow hunter, Traeger grill semi-pro (more semi than pro), former CrossFitter (emphasis on the former), and a whisky sommelier, which is real and just as douchy as it sounds.

Maybe the best way to know Garrett is from a few notes his wife wrote:

> A man who can only drink tequila under supervision.

> A man who will stop at nothing to provide his wife food if she gets HANGRY. Self-preservation, really.

> A dad who was totally cool with letting his sons go anywhere with him, in any costume they may have on! (Yeah, a client offered Garrett's kids $100 to knock on every door

in the neighborhood with him, sporting Spider-Man costumes and saying, "The neighborhood is safe." His costume was too small, and more Moose Knuckle Man than Spider-Man, but hey, that $100 spent the same.)

> A man who can't fix a toilet but can help you become financially independent so you can hire someone else to do it for you.

> A man who supports his wife's meditation, even if she is just sleeping.

> A brother who bailed his sister out of jail, while almost going to jail himself in the process.

> A father who loves and adores his sons for exactly who they are.

> A son who loves his parents with all his heart.

> A man loyal to his family and friends, but most of all to his values.